Finance
for Managers

The Harvard Business Essentials Series

The Harvard Business Essentials series is designed to provide comprehensive advice, personal coaching, background information, and guidance on the most relevant topics in business. Drawing on rich content from Harvard Business School Publishing and other sources, these concise guides are carefully crafted to provide a highly practical resource for readers with all levels of experience. To assure quality and accuracy, each volume is closely reviewed by a specialized content adviser from a world-class business school. Whether you are a new manager interested in expanding your skills or an experienced executive looking for a personal resource, these solution-oriented books offer reliable answers at your fingertips.

Other books in the series:

Hiring and Keeping the Best People
Managing Change and Transition

Finance
for Managers

Harvard Business School Press | *Boston, Massachusetts*

Library of Congress Cataloging-in-Publication Data
Finance for managers.
p. cm.—(The Harvard business essentials series) Includes index.
ISBN 1-57851-876-8 (alk. paper)
1. Corporations—Finance.   2. Business enterprises—Finance.   I. Series.
HG4026 .F494 2003
658.15—dc21
2002011667

Contents

Introduction

This book explains the essential concepts of finance to managers who are not financial managers. Whether you're in sales, marketing, manufacturing, product development, human resources, or some other operation, an understanding of financial concepts will help you do your job better and get ahead. And what's true for corporate managers is doubly true for the owners and managers of small businesses. Knowing how to finance assets, forecast future cash flows, maintain a budget, determine which operations are profit generators and which are not, and judge the real economic merits of different investment opportunities will help you stay in business and turn a profit.

Harvard Business Essentials—Finance for Managers explains the basics of this important subject. It will not make you a finance expert, nor will it qualify you to become a financial analyst, controller, or chief financial officer (CFO). But it will explain what you need to know to be an intelligent consumer of financial information, to plan, and to use financial concepts in making better business decisions.

The Big Picture of Business Finance

Reduced to its essentials, business finance is about acquiring and allocating resources—how a company goes about financing the assets it needs to run the business and how those assets can be put to their highest uses. In terms of acquiring resources, finance is concerned with questions such as these:

- How will the company acquire and finance its inventory, equipment, and other physical assets?

- Should it use the owners' money, borrowed funds, or internally generated cash for these acquisitions?

- If borrowing makes sense, which are the most appropriate sources of debt capital?

- Is leasing a superior alternative to owning?

- How long does it take to collect on the money owed by customers (accounts receivable)?

- How would profitability be affected if the company operated with a larger proportion of borrowed funds?

Now consider the allocation of resources. Here, finance addresses important questions such as these:

- If the enterprise had an opportunity to invest in two different ventures, how could it determine which would produce the greatest economic value in the years ahead?

- What return must a new activity produce in order to be worth undertaking? And how are returns measured, anyway?

- How many units of a new product or service must the company sell in order to break even on its investment?

- How can managers determine the profitability of the many different goods and services they produce?

Finance is also an information system. Drawing on the accounting function and its meticulous recording of transactions, finance produces numbers that managers can use to plan and control operations. These take the form of financial statements, budgets, and forecasts. Financial information gives managers the numbers they need to make better decisions—if they interpret and use those numbers correctly. One thing you'll learn here is how you can use financial information to determine which of your products or services are contributing to profits and which are not—something that is not always obvious.

What's Ahead

Chapters 1 and 2 of this book are concerned with financial statements: the balance sheet, income statement, and cash flow statement. These are the primary documents of finance. The first chapter explains these documents; the second shows you how to interpret them.

Chapter 3 covers a selected set of important accounting concepts, including accrual versus cash accounting, accounting for inventories and depreciation, the treatment of leases, the principle of historical cost, and cost accounting. This chapter won't make you an accountant, but it will help you understand some concepts that are very important for your business.

Taxes are the subject of chapter 4. The discussion is limited to business taxes, with particular emphasis on how the different forms of business organizations (proprietorships, partnerships, corporations, etc.) are uniquely taxed. If you are an entrepreneur faced with determining—or changing—how your business will be legally organized, this material will be particularly useful.

Both chapters 5 and 6 are concerned with financing operations and growth, and with the sources of debt and equity capital. Chapter 5 describes a typical life cycle of a successful business—from start-up, through growth, to maturity—and the financing sources that businesses tap at each phase. Chapter 6 describes the money and capital markets that growing businesses turn to as they become larger and more credible entities. Initial public offerings (IPOs), the role of investment bankers, and market securities are discussed.

Few enterprises function successfully without a good budget, the subject of chapter 7. Budgets are important tools for planning, coordinating, monitoring, and evaluating performance. This chapter provides a practical guide to budgeting, and explains step-by-step how you can create operating and cash budgets for your business or business unit.

Chapter 8 introduces financial tools you can use to make better decisions about internal and external investments. What is the return on investment on a new venture? How long will it take to recoup an investment? How many units will have to be sold at

specific prices to simply break even? Chapter 9 introduces even
more powerful tools for decision making: net present value and
internal rate of return. These tools are based on time value of
money concepts that you will find useful in many different spheres
of analysis and decision making.

Finally, chapter 10 is concerned with valuation. What is a business worth? How would you go about estimating the value of an
operating unit you planned to buy or sell? An important and technical subject, valuation is generally the province of experts. But like
every important business issue, it is too important to be left solely to
the experts. As a manager, you should be familiar with the different
valuation approaches, their strengths, and their weaknesses. You'll
find those different approaches here.

Like every discipline, finance has a unique vocabulary. Part of
the battle of mastering finance is simply understanding this language and becoming familiar with its use. At the back of the book,
you will find a glossary of all key terms. Each new term is italicized
when first introduced in the text, indicating that its definition can
be found in the glossary.

And if you'd like to learn more about any of the topics covered
in these chapters, we've provided a For Further Reading section, also
at the end of the book. There you'll find references to books, articles,
and, occasionally, to Harvard Business School classroom materials
that are publicly available at www.hbsp.harvard.edu.

In addition, the official Harvard Business Essentials Web site,
www.elearning.hbsp.org/businesstools, offers free interactive ver-
sions of the tools introduced in this series.

The content in this book is based on a number of books, articles,
and online productions of Harvard Business School Publishing, in
particular: Class notes prepared by William J. Bruns on accounting
and on reading and interpreting financial statements, by Michael J.
Roberts on the subjects of valuation techniques and business taxation of the various legal forms of business, and by Robert S. Kaplan
on the subject of activity-based costing; and modules on finance,
financial statements, and budgeting in Harvard ManageMentor®, an
online service.

1

Financial Statements

The Elements of Managerial Finance

Key Topics Covered in This Chapter

- *Balance sheets*

- *Income statements*

- *Cash flow statements*

- *Financial leverage*

- *The financial structure of the firm*

WHAT DOES YOUR COMPANY own, and what does it owe to others? What are its sources of revenue, and how has it spent its money? How much profit has it made? What is the state of your company's financial health? This chapter will help you answer those questions by explaining the three essential financial statements: the balance sheet, the income statement, and the cash flow statement. The chapter will also help you understand some of the managerial issues implicit in these statements and broaden your financial know-how through discussion of two important concepts: financial leverage, and the financial structure of the firm.

Why Financial Statements?

Financial statements are the essential documents of business. Executives use them to assess performance and identify areas in which managerial intervention is required. Shareholders use them to keep tabs of how well their capital is being managed. Outside investors use them to identify opportunities. And lenders and suppliers routinely examine financial statements to determine the creditworthiness of the companies with which they deal.

Publicly traded companies are required by the Securities and Exchange Commission (SEC) to produce financial statements and make them available to everyone as part of the full-disclosure

requirement the SEC places on publicly owned and traded companies. Companies not publicly traded are under no such requirement,
but their private owners and bankers expect financial statements
nevertheless.

Financial statements follow the same general format from company to company. And though specific line items may vary with the
nature of a company's business, the statements are usually similar
enough to allow you to compare one business's performance against
another's.

The Balance Sheet

Most people go to a doctor once a year to get a checkup—a snapshot of their physical well-being at a particular time. Similarly, companies prepare balance sheets as a way of summarizing their financial
positions at a given point in time, usually at the end of the month,
the quarter, or the fiscal year.

In effect, the balance sheet describes the assets controlled by the
business and how those assets are financed—with the funds of creditors (liabilities), with the capital of the owners, or with both. A balance sheet reflects the following basic accounting equation:

Assets = Liabilities + Owners' Equity

Assets in this equation are the things in which a company invests so
that it can conduct business. Examples include cash and financial
instruments, inventories of raw materials and finished goods, land,
buildings, and equipment. Assets also include moneys owed to the
company by customers and others—an asset category referred to as
accounts receivable.

Now look at the other side of the equation, starting with liabilities. To acquire its necessary assets, a company often borrows money
or promises to pay suppliers for various goods and services. Moneys
owed to creditors are called *liabilities*. For example, a computer company may acquire $1 million worth of motherboards from an elec-

tronic parts supplier, with payment due in thirty days. In doing so, the computer company increases its inventory assets by $1 million and its liabilities—in the form of *accounts payable*—by an equal amount. The equation stays in balance. Likewise, if the same company were to borrow $100,000 from a bank, the cash infusion would increase its assets by $100,000 and its liabilities by the same amount.

Owners' equity, also known as shareholders' or stockholders' equity, is what is left over after total liabilities are deducted from total assets. Thus, a company that has $3 million in total assets and $2 million in liabilities would have owners' equity of $1 million.

Assets − Liabilities = Owners' Equity

$3,000,000 − $2,000,000 = $1,000,000

If $500,000 of this same company's uninsured assets burned up in fire, its liabilities would remain the same, but its owners' equity— what's left after all claims against assets are satisfied—would be reduced to $500,000:

Assets − Liabilities = Owners' Equity

$2,500,000 − $2,000,000 = $500,000

Thus, the balance sheet "balances" a company's assets and liabilities. Notice, for instance, how total assets equal total liabilities and owners' equity in the balance sheet of Amalgamated Hat Rack, a company whose finances we will consider in many chapters of this book (table 1-1). The balance sheet also describes how much the company has invested in assets, and where the money is invested. Further, the balance sheet indicates how much of those monetary investments in assets comes from creditors (liabilities) and how much comes from owners (equity). Analysis of the balance sheet can give you an idea of how efficiently a company is utilizing its assets and how well it is managing its liabilities.

Balance sheet data is most helpful when compared with the same information from one or more previous years. Consider the

TABLE 1-1

Amalgamated Hat Rack Balance Sheet as of December 31, 2002

	2002	2001	Increase (Decrease)
Assets			
Cash and marketable securities	$355,000	$430,000	$(75,000)
Accounts receivable	$555,000	$512,000	$43,000
Inventory	$835,000	$755,000	$80,000
Prepaid expenses	$123,000	$98,000	$25,000
Total current assets	$1,868,000	$1,795,000	$73,000
Gross property, plant, and equipment	$2,100,000	$1,900,000	$200,000
Less: accumulated depreciation	$333,000	$234,000	$(99,000)
Net property, plant, and equipment	$1,767,000	$1,666,000	$101,000
Total assets	$3,635,000	$3,461,000	$174,000
Liabilities and Owner's Equity			
Accounts payable	$450,000	$430,000	$20,000
Accrued expenses	$98,000	$77,000	$21,000
Income tax payable	$17,000	$9,000	$8,000
Short-term debt	$435,000	$500,000	$(65,000)
Total current liabilities	$1,000,000	$1,016,000	$(16,000)
Long-term debt	$750,000	$660,000	$90,000
Total liabilities	$1,750,000	$1,676,000	$74,000
Contributed capital	$900,000	$850,000	$50,000
Retained earnings	$985,000	$935,000	$50,000
Total owner's equity	$1,885,000	$1,785,000	$100,000
Total liabilities and owner's equity	$3,635,000	$3,461,000	$174,000

Source: HMM Finance.

balance sheet of Amalgamated Hat Rack. First, this statement represents the company's financial position at a moment in time: December 31, 2002. A comparison of the figures for 2001 against those for
2002 shows that Amalgamated is moving in a positive direction: It
has increased its owners' equity by nearly $100,000.

Assets

You should understand some details about this particular financial
statement. The balance sheet begins by listing the assets most easily
converted to cash: cash on hand and marketable securities, receivables, and inventory. These are called *current assets*. Generally, current
assets are those that can be converted into cash within one year.

Next, the balance sheet tallies other assets that are tougher to
convert to cash—for example, buildings and equipment. These are
called plant assets or, more commonly, *fixed assets* (because it is hard
to change them into cash).

Since most fixed assets, except land, depreciate—or become less
valuable—over time, the company must reduce the stated value of
these fixed assets by something called accumulated depreciation.
Gross property, plant, and equipment minus accumulated depreciation equals the current book value of property, plant, and equipment.

Some companies list *goodwill* among their assets. If a company
has purchased another company for a price above the fair market
value of its assets, that so-called goodwill is recorded as an asset. This
is, however, strictly an accounting fiction. Goodwill may also represent intangible things such as brand names or the acquired company's excellent reputation. These may have real value. So too can
other intangible assets, such as patents.

Finally, we come to the last line of the balance sheet, total assets.
Total assets represents the sum of both current and fixed assets.

Liabilities and Owners' Equity

Now let's consider the claims against those assets, beginning with a
category called current liabilities. *Current liabilities* represent the
claims of creditors and others that typically must be paid within a

year; they include short-term IOUs, accrued salaries, accrued income taxes, and accounts payable. This year's repayment obligation on a long-term loan is also listed under current liabilities.

Subtracting current liabilities from current assets gives you the company's net working capital. *Net working capital* is the amount of money the company has tied up in its current (i.e., short-term) operating activities. Just how much is adequate for the company depends on the industry and the company's plans. In its most recent balance sheet, Amalgamated had $868,000 in net working capital.

Long-term liabilities are typically bonds and mortgages—debts that the company is contractually obliged to repay, with respect to both interest and principal.

According to the aforementioned accounting equation, total assets must equal total liabilities plus owners' equity. Thus, subtracting total liabilities from total assets, the balance sheet arrives at a figure for the owners' equity. Owners' equity comprises *retained earnings* (net profits that accumulate on a company's balance sheet after any dividends are paid) and contributed capital (capital received in exchange for shares).

Historical Values

The values represented in many balance sheet categories may not correspond to their actual market values. Except for items such as cash, accounts receivable, and accounts payable, the measurement of each classification will rarely be equal to the actual current value shown. This is because accountants must record most items at their historic cost. If, for example, XYZ's balance sheet indicated land worth $700,000, that figure would represent what XYZ paid for the land way back when. If the land was purchased in downtown San Francisco in 1960, you can bet that it is now worth immensely more than the value stated on the balance sheet. So why do accountants use historic instead of market values? The short answer is that it represents the lesser of two evils. If market values were required, then every public company would be required to get a professional appraisal of every one of it properties, warehouse inventories, and so forth—and would have to do so every year. And how many people would trust those appraisals? So we're stuck with historic values on the balance sheet.

Managerial Issues

Though the balance sheet is prepared by accountants, it represents a number of important issues for managers.

WORKING CAPITAL. Financial managers give substantial attention to the level of working capital, which naturally expands and contracts with sales activities. Too little working capital can put a company in a bad position: The company may be unable to pay its bills or to take advantage of profitable opportunities. Too much working capital, on the other hand, reduces profitability since that capital has a carrying cost—it must be financed in some way, usually through interest-bearing loans.

Inventory is one component of working capital that directly affects many non-financial managers. Like working capital in general, there's a tension between having too much and too little inventory. Having lots of inventory on hand solves many business problems: The company can fill customer orders without delay, and a robust inventory provides a buffer against potential production stoppages and strikes. The flip side of plentiful inventory is financing cost and the risk of a deterioration in the market value of the inventory itself. Every excess widget in the stockroom adds to the company's financing costs, which reduces profits. And every item that sits on the shelf may become obsolete or less salable as time goes by—again, with a negative impact on profitability.

The personal computer business provides a clear example of how excess inventory can wreck the bottom line. Some analysts estimate that the value of finished-goods inventory melts away at a rate of approximately 2 percent *per day*, because of technical obsolescence in this fast-moving industry. Inventory meltdown really hammered Apple during the mid-1990s, before it dramatically reduced its inventories through operational redesign. Apple had exceptional products and hard-core fans, but finished 1996 with almost $700 million tied up in inventory. Bulging inventories wreaked havoc on Apple's bottom line, as obsolete components and finished goods had to be dumped onto the market at huge discounts. By comparison, its rival, Dell, operated with *no* finished-goods inventory and with negligible stocks of components. Dell's success formula was an ultrafast supply-chain/assembly system that quickly assembled PCs to customer specifications as those orders were received. Nothing was built until the company had a specified customer order in hand. Finished Dell PCs didn't end up on stockroom shelves for weeks at a time, but went directly from the assembly line into waiting delivery trucks. The profit lesson to managers is very clear: Shape your operations to minimize or eliminate inventories.

FINANCIAL LEVERAGE. You have probably heard someone say, "It's a highly leveraged situation." Do you know what "leveraged" means in the financial sense? *Financial leverage* refers to the use of borrowed money in acquiring an asset. We say that a company is highly leveraged when the percentage of debt on its balance sheet is high relative to the capital invested by the owners. For example, suppose that you paid $400,000 for an asset, using $100,000 of your own money and $300,000 in borrowed funds. For simplicity, we'll ignore loan payments, taxes, and any cash flow you might get from the investment. Four years go by, and your asset has appreciated to $500,000. You decide to sell. After paying off the $300,000 loan, you end up with $200,000 in your pocket (your original $100,000 plus a $100,000 profit). That's a gain of 100 percent on your personal capital, even though the asset increased in value by only 25 percent. Financial leverage made this possible. In contrast, if you had financed the purchase entirely with your own funds ($400,000), then you would have ended up with only a 25 percent gain. (*Operating leverage,* in contrast, refers to the extent to which a company's operating costs are fixed versus variable. For example, a company that relies heavily on machinery and very few workers to produce its goods has a high operating leverage.)

Where Are the Human Assets?

As people look to financial statements to gain insights about companies, many are questioning the traditional balance sheet's ability to reflect the value of human capital and profit potential. This is particularly true for knowledge-intensive companies, for which the work-force know-how, intellectual property, brand equity, and customer relationships are the real productive assets. Unfortunately, these intangible assets are not found on the balance sheet.

The growing inability of balance sheets to reflect real value prompted Federal Reserve Board Chairman Alan Greenspan to complain in January 2000 that accounting failed to track investments in "knowledge assets." Former SEC chairman, Arthur Levitt, echoed Greenspan's concern: "As intangible assets grow in size and scope, more and more people are questioning whether the true value—and the drivers of that value—are being reflected in a timely manner in publicly available disclosure." Indeed, a study by Baruch Lev of New York University found that 40 percent of the market valuation of the average company was missing from its balance sheet." For high-tech firms, the figure was more than 50 percent.

The implication of these findings for investors and managers is that they must look beyond the bricks and mortar, the equipment, and even the cash, that traditionally constitute balance sheet assets and focus on the undisclosed assets that produce the greatest value for shareholders. In most cases, those assets are the people who create the bonds between the enterprise and its customers, who create innovations that people are eager to pay for, and who know how to get others to work together productively. The accounting profession is beginning to debate the pros and cons of including these intangible assets in financial statements. Watch for future developments.

Financial leverage creates an opportunity for a company to gain a higher return on the capital invested by its owners. In the United States and most other countries, tax policy makes financial leverage even more attractive by allowing businesses to deduct the interest paid on loans. But leverage can cut both ways. If the value of an asset drops (or fails to produce the anticipated level of revenue), then leverage works against its owner. Consider what would have happened in our example if the asset's value had dropped by $100,000, that is, to $300,000. The owner would have lost his or her entire $100,000 investment after repaying the initial loan of $300,000.

FINANCIAL STRUCTURE OF THE FIRM. The negative potential of financial leverage is what keeps CEOs, their financial executives, and board members from maximizing their debt financing. Instead, they seek a financial structure that creates a realistic balance between debt and equity on the balance sheet. Although leverage enhances a company's potential profitability as long as things go right, managers know that every dollar of debt increases the riskiness of the business—both because of the danger just cited, and because high debt results in high interest payments, which must be paid in good times and bad. Many companies have failed when business reversals or recessions reduced their ability to make timely payments on their loans.

When creditors and investors examine corporate balance sheets, they look carefully at the debt-to-equity ratio. They factor the riskiness of the balance sheet into the interest they charge on loans and the return they demand from a company's bonds. Thus, a highly leveraged company may have to pay 14 percent on borrowed funds instead of 10 to 12 percent paid by a less leveraged competitor. Investors also demand a higher rate of return for their stock investments in highly leveraged companies. They will not accept high risks without an expectation of commensurately large returns.

The Income Statement

The income statement indicates the results of operations over a *specified period*. Those last two words are important. Unlike the balance sheet, which is a snapshot of the enterprise's position *at a point in time,* the income statement indicates cumulative business results within a defined time frame. It tells you if the company is making a profit—that is, whether it has positive or negative net income (net earnings). This is why the income statement is often referred to as the *profit-and-loss statement,* or P&L. It shows a company's profitability at the end of a particular time—typically at the end of the month, the quarter, or the company's fiscal year. In addition, the income statement tells you how much money the company spent to make that profit—from which you can determine the company's *profit margin.*

As we did with the balance sheet, we can represent the contents of the income statement with a simple equation:

Revenues − Expenses = Net Income (or Net Loss)

An income statement starts with the company's *revenues:* the amount of money that results from selling products or services to customers. A company may have other revenues as well. In many cases, these are from investments or interest income from its cash holdings.

Various costs and expenses—from the costs of making and storing a company's goods, to depreciation of plant and equipment, to interest expense and taxes—are then deducted from revenues. The bottom line—what's left over—is the *net income,* or *net profit* or *net earnings,* for the period of the statement.

Consider the meaning of various line items on the income statement for Amalgamated Hat Rack (table 1-2). The *cost of goods sold* is what it costs Amalgamated to manufacture its hat racks. This figure includes the cost of raw materials, such as lumber, as well as the cost of turning them into finished goods, including direct labor costs. By deducting the cost of goods sold from sales revenue, we get a company's *gross profit*—the roughest estimation of the company's profitability.

The next major category of cost is *operating expenses.* Operating expenses include administrative employee salaries, rents, sales and

TABLE 1-2

Amalgamated Hat Rack Income Statement for the Fiscal Year Ending December 31, 2002

Retail Sales	$2,200,000
Corporate Sales	$1,000,000
Total Sales Revenue	$3,200,000
Less: Cost of Goods Sold	$1,600,000
Gross Profit	$1,600,000
Less: Operating Expenses	$800,000
Depreciation Expense	$42,500
Earnings before Interest and Taxes	$757,500
Less: Interest Expense	$110,000
Earnings before Income Tax	$647,500
Less: Income Tax	$300,000
Net Income	$347,500

Source: HMM Finance.

marketing costs, as well as other costs of business not directly attributed to the cost of manufacturing a product. The lumber for making
hat racks would *not* be included here; the cost of the advertising and
the salaries of Amalgamated employees would.

Depreciation is counted on the income statement as an expense,
even though it involves no out-of-pocket payments. As described
earlier, depreciation is a way of estimating the "consumption" of an
asset, or the diminishing value of equipment, over time. A computer,
for example, loses about a third of its value each year. Thus, the company would not expense the full value of a computer in the first year

of its purchase, but as it is actually used over a span of three years. The idea behind depreciation is to lay aside enough money to eventually replace a worn-out asset.

By subtracting operating expenses and depreciation from the gross profit, we get *operating earnings.* These earnings are often called *earnings before interest and taxes,* or EBIT.

We're now down to the last reductions in the path that revenues follow on their way to the bottom line. Interest expense is the interest charged on loans a company has taken out. Income tax, tax levied by the government on corporate income, is the final charge.

What revenues are left are referred to as net income, or earnings. If net income is positive—as it is in the case of Amalgamated—we have a profit, what the for-profit company lives for.

Making Sense of the Income Statement

As with the balance sheet, our analysis of a company's income statement is greatly aided when presented in a multiperiod format. This allows us to spot trends and turnarounds. Most annual reports make multiperiod data available, often going back five or more years. Amalgamated's income statement in multiperiod form is depicted in table 1–3.

In this multiyear format, we observe that Amalgamated's annual retail sales have grown steadily, while its corporate sales have stagnated and even declined slightly. Operating expenses have stayed about the same, however, even as total sales have expanded. That's a good sign that management is holding the line on the cost of doing business. The company's interest expense has also declined, perhaps because it has paid off one of its loans. The bottom line, net income, has shown healthy growth.

The Cash Flow Statement

The *cash flow statement,* the last of the three essential financial statements, is also the least used and understood. The statement details

TABLE 1-3

Amalgamated Hat Rack Multiperiod Income Statement

| | FOR THE PERIOD ENDING DECEMBER 31 | | | |
	2002	2001	2000	1999
Retail Sales	$2,200,000	$2,000,000	$1,720,000	$1,500,000
Corporate Sales	$1,000,000	$1,000,000	$1,100,000	$1,200,000
Total Sales Revenue	$3,200,000	$3,000,000	$2,820,000	$2,700,000
Less: Cost of Goods Sold	$1,600,000	$1,550,000	$1,400,000	$1,300,000
Gross Profit	$1,600,000	$1,450,000	$1,420,000	$1,400,000
Less: Operating Expenses	$800,000	$810,000	$812,000	$805,000
Depreciation Expense	$42,500	$44,500	$45,500	$42,500
Earnings before Interest and Taxes	$757,500	$595,500	$562,500	$552,500
Less: Interest Expense	$110,000	$110,000	$150,000	$150,000
Earnings before Income Tax	$647,500	$485,500	$412,500	$402,500
Less: Income Tax	$300,000	$194,200	$165,000	$161,000
Net Income	$347,500	$291,300	$247,500	$241,500

the reasons why the amount of cash (and cash equivalents) changed during the accounting period. More specifically, it reflects all changes in cash as affected by operating activities, investments, and financing activities. Like the bank statement you receive for your checking account, the cash flow statement tells how much cash was on hand at the beginning of the period, and how much was on hand at the end. It then describes how the company acquired and spent cash in a particular period. The uses of cash are recorded as negative figures, and sources of cash are recorded as positive figures.

If you're a manager in a large corporation, changes in the company's cash flow won't typically have an impact on your day-to-day functioning. Nevertheless, it's a good idea to stay up to date with your company's cash flow projections, because they may come into play when you prepare your budget for the upcoming year. For example, if cash is tight, you will probably want to be conservative in your spending. Alternatively, if the company is flush with cash, you may have opportunities to make new investments. If you're a manager in a small company or its owner, you're probably keenly aware of your cash flow situation and feel its impact almost every day.

The cash flow statement is useful because it indicates whether your company is turning accounts receivable into cash—and that ability is ultimately what will keep your company solvent. *Solvency* is the ability to pay bills as they come due.

As we did with the other statements, we can conceptualize the cash flow statement in terms of a simple equation:

Cash Flow from Profit + Other Sources of Cash − Uses of Cash =
Change in Cash

Again using the Amalgamated Hat Rack example, we see that in its year 2002 cash flow statement, the company generated a positive cash flow of $377,900 (table 1-4). The statement shows that cash flows from operations ($283,900), plus those from investing activities ($92,000), and from financing ($2,000) produced $377,000 in additional cash.

The cash flow statement doesn't measure the same thing as the income statement. If there is no cash transaction, then it cannot be reflected on a cash flow statement. Notice, however, that net income at the top of the cash flow statement is the same as the bottom line of the income statement—it's the company's profit. Through a series of adjustments, the cash flow statement translates this net income into a cash basis.

The statement's format reflects the three categories of activities that affect cash. Cash can be increased or decreased because of (1) operations, (2) the acquisition or sale of assets, that is, investments, or

TABLE 1-4

Amalgamated Hat Rack Cash Flow Statement, 2002

Net Income	$347,500
Operating Assets and Liabilities	
Accounts receivable	$(75,600)
Finished-goods inventory	$(125,000)
Prepaid expenses	$(37,000)
Accounts payable	$83,000
Accrued expenses	$25,000
Income tax payable	$(23,000)
Depreciation expense	$89,000
Total changes in operating assets and liabilities	$(63,600)
Cash flow from operations	$283,900
Investing Activities	
Sale of property, plant, and equipment	$267,000
Capital expenditures	$(175,000)
Cash flow from investing activities	$92,000
Financing Activities	
Short-term debt increase	$27,000
Long-term borrowing	$112,000
Capital stock	$50,000
Cash dividends to stockholders	$(187,000)
Cash flow from financing activities	$2,000
Increase in cash during year	$377,900

Source: HMM Finance.

(3) changes in debt or stock or other financing activities. Let's consider each in turn, starting with operations:

- Accounts receivable and finished–goods inventory represent items the company has produced, but for which it hasn't received payment. Prepaid expenses represent items the company has paid for but has not consumed. These items are all subtracted from cash flow.

- Accounts payable and accrued expenses represent items the company has already received or used, but for which it hasn't yet paid. Consequently, these items add to cash flow.

Now, consider investments. Investment activities include the following:

- Gains realized from the sale of plant, property, and equipment

- Cash that the company uses to invest in financial instruments and plant, property, and equipment (such investments in plant, property, and equipment are often shown as capital expenditures)

The cash flow statement shows that Amalgamated has sold a building for $267,000 and made capital expenditures of $175,000 for a net addition to cash flow of $92,000.

Finally, we come to cash flow changes from financing activities. Amalgamated has raised money by increasing its short–term debt, by borrowing in the capital markets, and by issuing capital stock, thereby increasing its available cash flow. The dividends that Amalgamated pays, however ($187,000), must be paid out of cash flow and thus represent a decrease in cash flow.

Where to Find It

As mentioned earlier, all firms that trade their shares in U.S. public financial markets are required by the Securities and Exchange Commission (SEC) to prepare and distribute their financial statements in

Cash Flow versus Profit

Many people think of profits as cash flow. Don't make this mistake. For a particular period, profit may or may not contribute positively to cash flow. For example, if this year's profit derives from a huge sale made in November, the sale may be booked as revenues in the fiscal period—thus adding to profit. But if payment for that sale is not received until the next accounting period, it goes on the books as an account receivable, which reduces cash flow.

an annual report to shareholders. Most annual reports go beyond the basic disclosure requirement of the SEC, providing discussion of the year's operations and the future outlook. Most public companies also issue quarterly reports.

If you are looking for even more material on your company—or on one of your competitors—obtain a copy of the company's annual Form 10-K. The 10-K often contains abundant and revealing information about a company's strategy, its view of the market and its customers, its products, its important risks and business challenges, and so forth. You can obtain 10-K reports and annual and quarterly reports directly from a company's investor relations department, or online at http://www.sec.gov/edgar/searchedgar/formpick.htm.

Summing Up

This chapter has introduced and explained the balance sheet, income statement, and cash flow statement. These statements offer three perspectives on your company's financial performance. They tell three different but related stories about how well your company is doing financially:

- The balance sheet shows a company's financial position at a specific point in time. That is, it gives a snapshot of the company's financial situation—its assets, equity, and liabilities—on a given day.

- The income statement shows the bottom line: It indicates how much profit or loss was generated over a period—a month, a quarter, or a year.

- The cash flow statement tells where the company's cash came from and where it went—in other words, the flow of cash in, through, and out of the company.

Here is another way to look at the interrelationships between these statements: The income statement tells you whether your company is making a profit. The balance sheet tells you how efficiently a company is utilizing its assets and managing its liabilities in pursuit of profits. The cash flow statement tells you how cash has been increased or decreased through operations, the acquisition or sale of assets, and financing activities.

Together, these financial statements can help you understand what is going on in your company or any other business. Chapter 2 will show you how you can gain even more business insights through various forms of analysis.

Finding Meaning in Financial Statements

A Look behind the Numbers

Key Topics Covered in This Chapter

- *Profitability, key activities, and solvency*

- *Comparing the financial statements of different entities*

- *Balanced scorecards*

CHAPTER 1 EXPLAINED the three key financial statements and their various components. Chapter 2 provides you with tools for interpreting those statements and assessing business performance. Additionally, it introduces a relatively new approach to gauging a business's nonfinancial aspects that ultimately foreshadow financial performance.

Ratio Analysis

Many people use financial statements, and often for very different reasons. Lenders want to know if a company seeking funds has the capacity to repay them. Investors are interested in financial stability and profit-generating power and how earnings are likely to grow or diminish in the future. Many potential employees use financial statements to assess the current performance or financial status of an enterprise before they sign on with a company. Regulatory agencies often need to assess organizational or industry financial health and performance.

Each of these uses of financial statements is a form of financial analysis. Financial analysis often involves an examination of the relationships, or ratios, between items found in financial statements.[1] These ratios help describe the financial condition of an organization, the efficiency of its activities, its comparable profitability, and the perception of investors as expressed by their behavior in financial markets. Ratios help an analyst or decision maker piece together a story about where an organization has come from, its current condition, and its possible future. In most cases, the story told by these ratios is incomplete, but it's a start. The ratios that follow are relevant across a wide spectrum of industries, but are most meaningful when compared against the same measures for other companies in the same industry.

Profitability Ratios

Profitability ratios associate the amount of income earned with the resources used to generate it. Ideally, the firm should produce as much income as possible from a given amount of resources. The profitability ratios to remember are *return on assets* (ROA), *return on equity* (ROE), and *earnings per share* (EPS). Also discussed is the "return on investment" (ROI), a much-used, and much-abused, piece of financial terminology.

Return on assets relates net income to the company's total asset base and is figured as follows:

ROA = Net Income / Total Assets

ROA relates net income to the investment in all the financial resources at the command of management. It is most useful as a measure of effective resource utilization—without regard to how those resources were obtained or financed. Analysts and investors often compare the ROA of one company to the ROA of its peer group of key competitors to assess the effectiveness of top management. For example, if company A has an ROA of 12 percent and company B has 8 percent, then this says something positive about company A's management.

Return on equity relates net income to the amount invested by shareholders. It is a measure of how efficiently the shareholders' stake in the business has been used. ROE is calculated as follows:

ROE = Net Income / Shareholders' Equity

"Return on investment" is often used in business discussions that involve profitability. For example, expressions like "We aim for an ROI of 12 percent" are common. Unfortunately, there is no standard definition of ROI, since "investment" may be construed from many perspectives. Investment might represent the assets committed to a particular activity, the shareholders' equity involved, or invested assets minus any liabilities generated by a company's taking on a project. ROI might also refer to the internal rate of return, a very specific calculation of return described in chapter 8. So, when someone uses the term "return on investment," *always* get a clarification. Ask, "How are you calculating investment?"

The earnings-before-interest-and-taxes margin (EBIT margin), more generally known as the *operating margin,* is used by many analysts to gauge the profitability of a company's operating activities. The operating margin removes from the equation the interest expenses and taxes over which current management may have no control, thus giving a clearer indicator of management performance. To calculate the operating margin, use this formula:

Operating Margin = EBIT / Net Sales

Corporations generally have many owners, not all of whom own an equal number of shares. For this reason it is common to express earnings on a per-share basis. The calculation of *earnings per share,* or EPS, can be complicated if there is more than one class of ownership, each with different claims against the income and assets of the firm.[2] The earnings-per-share ratio must be presented in published reports, often in several variations, such as "primary" or "fully diluted" EPS. A simplified formula that contains all the elements for determining earnings per share is this:

Fully Diluted EPS = (Net Income − Preferred Stock Dividends) / (Number of Common Shares + Equivalents)

The *profit margin*—sometimes called the *return on sales,* or ROS—indicates a rate of return on sales. It tells us what percentage of every dollar of sales makes it to the bottom line. The profit margin is calculated as follows:

Profit Margin = Net Income / Net Sales

Both managers and investors watch the trend in profit margin closely. A rising percentage indicates either that customers are accepting higher prices or that management is doing a better job of controlling costs and expenses, or both. On the other hand, a declining profit margin may be a signal that management is losing control of its costs, or that the company is having to "give away the store" in the form of discounts to sell its products or services.

The profit margin trend for our fictional company, Amalgamated Hat Rack, shows a precipitous drop in year 2002:

2002	2001	2000	1999
10.9%	20.1%	17.4%	17.3%

Why did the company's margin drop almost in half between 2001 and 2002? One way to narrow down the possible answers is to determine which categories of cost or expense—or taxes—have increased relative to sales revenues. For instance, examination of the company's income statements, and a little calculating, indicates that the company paid more taxes relative to sales in 2002 than in the previous year (9.4 percent versus 6.5 percent). We could also look at the cost of goods sold or operating expenses with the same methodology in seeking the answer. These, unlike taxes, represent areas over which management has significant control.

Investors use profitability analysis to gauge a company's future earning power. As the example shows, managers can use it to identify areas where performance is being inhibited—so that they can take corrective action.

Activity Ratios

Activity ratios provide an indication of how well an organization utilizes its assets. The efficient use of assets minimizes the need for investment by lenders and owners. Less investment means both lower risk and lower cost. Two activity ratios that many managers must deal with regularly are *days receivables outstanding* and *inventory turnover*.

Days receivables outstanding (sometimes called the collection period) tells us the average time it takes to collect on sales made by the company. As discussed, a longer collection period means that more working capital is required to run the business—working capital whose interest charges put a drain on profits! We find days receivables outstanding through two steps. The first determines the average day's sales:

Average Day's Sales = Net Sales / 365

We use this result to reach our final goal:

Days Receivables Outstanding = Accounts Receivable / Average Day's Sales

As with most forms of ratio analysis, days of receivables outstanding provides the greatest insights when we use it to (1) compare one company with another or with its peer group of industry rivals or (2) to examine a trend. For example, Gateway and rival Dell are both make-to-order manufacturers of personal computers. Both sell directly to customers. Their business models are very similar. Thus, a comparison of days receivables outstanding would tell us which company is more effective in collecting the money owed to it. Likewise, we could examine the trend of days receivables in either or both companies to determine whether the collection period was becoming shorter or longer.

Inventory turnover is another ratio that concerns many managers. Determining the number of times that inventory is sold and replaced during the year provides some measure of its liquidity and the ability of the company to convert inventories to cash quickly if that were to become necessary. Slow turnover may point to too much capital tied up in inventory. Such capital costs money and, in areas such as technology and apparel, can result in inventory obsolescence. Profits improve when you can move inventory out the door quickly.

You can calculate inventory turnover by dividing the cost of goods sold by the inventory cost. If inventory cost has significantly changed from the beginning to the end of the period, you should calculate or estimate an average inventory for the period. Usually you can simply add the beginning and ending inventory amounts and use one-half of that total as the average inventory for the period. Here is the formula:

Inventory Turnover = Cost of Goods Sold / Average Inventory

What level of inventory turnover represents effective management? There is no universal answer to this question, as inventory turnover is essentially industry-specific. In the retail grocery business, for example, inventory turnover is extremely high—items that come into the receiving dock in the morning usually go out the front door in shopping bags by the end of the same day. An auto dealer, in contrast, may only turn his inventory once every few weeks. A retailer of fine musical instruments may turn her inventory only three or four times each year. Thus, it's again important to examine the turnover rate trend and how one enterprise stacks up against its industry rivals.

Solvency Ratios

When an organization is unable to meet its financial obligations (i.e., when it cannot pay its bills), it is said to be insolvent. Because insolvency leads to organizational distress, possibly to bankruptcy, or even to liquidation of the business, investors and creditors closely scrutinize solvency ratios. By measuring a company's ability to meet financial obligations as they become due, solvency ratios give an indication of its liquidity. The term *liquidity* in finance refers to the extent to which a company's assets can readily be turned into cash for meeting current obligations. The *current ratio* and *acid test ratio* are commonly used for this measurement.

The current-ratio formula is simple:

Current Ratio = Current Assets / Current Liabilities

The size of the current ratio that a healthy company needs to maintain depends on the relationship between inflows of cash and the
demands for cash payments. A company that has a continuous and
reliable inflow of cash or other liquid assets, such as a public utility or
taxi company, may be able to meet currently maturing obligations
easily despite a small current ratio—say, 1.10 (which means that the
company has $1.10 in current assets for every $1.00 of current
liabilities). On the other hand, a manufacturing firm with long
product development and manufacturing cycles may need to maintain a larger current ratio.

To confirm the absolute liquidity of an organization, an analyst
can modify the current ratio by eliminating from current assets all
that cannot be liquidated on very short notice. Typically then, this
ratio, called the acid-test ratio, consists of the ratio of so-called quick
assets (cash, marketable security, and accounts receivable) to current
liabilities. Inventory is left out of the calculation.

Acid-Test Ratio = Quick Assets / Current Liabilities

Paradoxically, a company can have loads of choice assets—office
buildings, fleets of delivery trucks, and warehouses brimming with
finished-goods inventory—and still risk insolvency if its ratio of current (or quick) assets is insufficient to meet bills as they come due.
Creditors don't take payment in used delivery trucks; they want
cash.

As discussed earlier, the degree to which the activities of a company are supported by liabilities and long-term debt as opposed to
owners' contributions is called leverage. A firm that has a high proportion of debt relative to shareholder contributions is said to be
highly leveraged. For owners, the advantage of having high debt is
that returns on their actual investments can be disproportionately
higher when the company makes a profit. On the other hand, high
leverage is a negative when cash flows fall, since the interest on debt
is a contractual obligation—it must be paid in bad times as well as
good. A company can be forced into bankruptcy by the crush of
interest payments due on its outstanding debt.

The debt ratio is widely used in financial analysis because it reveals the effect of financial leverage. It is calculated in different ways, two of which are illustrated here. The simplest is this:

Debt Ratio = Total Debt / Total Assets

Alternatively, you can calculate the debt-to-equity ratio by dividing the total liabilities by the amount of shareholders' equity:

Debt-to-Equity Ratio = Total Liabilities / Owners' Equity

Analysts must use care when interpreting either of these ratios because there is no absolutely correct debt measure. So when you hear someone say, "The company's debt-to-equity ratio is one-to-two (or 50 percent)," you should ask what he or she has included as debt. Fully funded debt, that is, all the debt that carries an interest rate charge, is probably the best measure of debt.

In general, as the ratio increases, the returns to owners are higher, but so too are the risks. Creditors understand this relationship extremely well and will often include specific limits on the debt levels beyond which borrowers may not go without having their loans called in.

Creditors also use the *times interest earned ratio* to estimate how safe it is to lend money to individual businesses. Almost every firm has continuing commitments that must be met by future cash flows if the company is to remain solvent. Interest payments are one of those commitments. The ratio that measures the ability of a company to meet its interest payments is times interest earned. The formula for this ratio is:

Times Interest Earned Ratio = Earnings before Interest and Taxes / Interest Expense

The number of times that interest payments are covered by pre-tax earnings, or EBIT, indicates the degree to which income could fall without causing insolvency. In many cases, this is not so much a test of solvency as a test of staying power under adversity. For example, if EBIT were to be cut in half because of a recession or another cause, would the company still have sufficient earnings to meet its interest obligations?

A Caveat on Ratio Analysis

Though the analyst or decision maker is better informed through ratio analysis, the indiscriminate use of financial ratios can be dangerous. Decisions based solely on a specific or minimum level of a ratio can easily lead to missed opportunities or losses. Even the best ratio is not always indicative of the finance health, status, or performance of an organization. Ratios between apparently similar measurements in financial statements may be affected by differences in accounting practices or by deliberate manipulation.

The ease with which ratios can be manipulated and the danger in using them as criteria lead many analysts to concentrate on ratio trends. When you observe a trend in a ratio, you can raise questions about why the trend is occurring. For example, if the quarter-to-quarter current ratio has been steadily increasing, you'll want to know why—and its implications. The answers to these questions are often found outside the financial statements. Likewise, simply comparing firms on their ratios can give erroneous conclusions. The diversity inherent in the available accounting practices can mean that the ratios of different organizations are noncomparable. You can make comparisons between companies, but you must make them with care and with full attention to the underlying differences in accounting methods.

Percentage–Format Financial Statements

To get a better handle on a firm's changing performance over time, and to compare one firm with another, many analysts create financial statements in which the balance sheet and income statements are prepared in a percentage format. In a percentage-format balance sheet, for example, each asset, liability, and owners' equity amount is expressed as a percentage of total assets. In a percentage-format statement of income, sales revenues are set at 100 percent, and each item is expressed as a percentage of sales. For example, cost of goods sold might be expressed as 40 percent of sales; net income might be 10 percent of sales.

Financial statements expressed in percentage form facilitate the comparison of different-sized firms, allowing analysts to focus on the efficiency of operations. For example, in comparing rival firms in the same industry, you can use percentage-format balance sheets to answer several key questions:

- Which firm has the highest percentage of debt to total assets?

- Which firm is holding the greatest amount of inventory relative to total assets?

- Which has a greater percentage of its assets tied up in fixed assets such as land, property, and equipment?

You can make other comparisons of firms using a percentage-format income statement. Perhaps as useful is the comparison of the same firm's income statement performance from year to year. For an example, consider the income statement in table 2-1. This three-year income statement indicates that the company's cost of goods relative to net sales is on an even keel. Its selling, general, and administrative expenses as a percentage of sales are likewise steady over the three-year period.

As an analyst, you're looking for indicators that something is going very right or very wrong in these numbers, which we don't see in this particular case. For example, if the selling, general, and administrative costs, as percentages, were in an upward trend, then you'd want to know why. As a manager, you would want to know the root cause and would want to take action to reverse the trend.

From Financial Measures to a Balanced Scorecard

Financial measures such as earnings per share and profit margin tell the tale of business performance, and generations of businesspeople have tried to manage using these measures. But these traditional measures aren't buttons that we can push to make things happen—

TABLE 2-1

Percentage Format Income Statement

	2001	2000	1999
Net Sales	100.0%	100.0%	100.0%
Cost of sales	37.4	36.6	37.8
Gross Profit	62.6%	63.4%	62.2%
Selling, general, and administrative expenses	42.4	43.2	42.1
Realignment expense	=	=	4.9
Profit from Operations	20.2%	20.2%	15.2%
Nonoperating charges (income)			
Interest income	(.1)%	(.3)%	(.5)%
Interest expense	.8	1.0	1.1
Other charges - net	.4	1.3	2.0
	1.1%	2.0%	2.6%
Income before Income Taxes and Cumulative Effect of Accounting Changes	19.1%	18.2%	12.6%
Income taxes	7.0	6.7	4.7
Income before Cumulative Effect of Accounting Changes	12.1%	11.5%	7.9%
Cumulative effect of accounting changes	=	=	(2.6)
Net Income	12.1%	11.5%	5.3%

Source: William J. Bruns, Jr., "Introduction to Financial Ratios and Financial Statement Analysis," Case 9-193-029 (Boston: Harvard Business School, revised August 21, 1996.)

they are outcomes of dozens of other activities. And they are back-ward-looking, the products of past activities. Worse, traditional measures can send the wrong signals. For instance, profit measures that look very good this year may be the result of dramatic cuts in new-product development and reductions in employee training. On the surface, they make the state of affairs look rosy, but these cuts jeop-ardize tomorrow's profits.

Frustrated by the inadequacies of traditional performance measurement systems, some managers have shifted their focus from earnings per share and return on equity to the operational activities that produce them. These managers follow the motto "Make operational improvements, and the performance numbers will follow." But which improvements are the most important? Which are the true drivers of long-term, bottom-line performance? To answer these questions, Robert Kaplan and David Norton conducted research on a number of companies with leading-edge performance measures. From this research, they developed a so-called balanced scorecard, a new performance measurement system that gives top managers a fast but comprehensive view of the business. Their balanced scorecard includes financial measures that indicate the results of past actions. And it complements those financial measures with three sets of operational measures that relate directly to customer satisfaction, internal processes, and the organization's ability to learn and improve—the activities that drive future financial performance.

Kaplan and Norton have compared the balanced scorecard to the dials and indicators in an airplane cockpit: "For the complex task of navigating and flying an airplane, pilots need detailed information about many aspects of the flight. They need information on fuel, air speed, altitude, bearing, destination, and other indicators that summarize the current and predicted environment. Reliance on one instrument can be fatal. Similarly, the complexity of managing an organization today requires that managers be able to view performance in several areas simultaneously."[3]

Kaplan and Norton's balanced scorecard uses four perspectives to link performance measures and to galvanize managerial action. Collectively, these perspectives give top management timely answers to four key questions:

- How do customers see us? (customer perspective)

- What must we do to excel? (internal perspective)

- Can we continue to improve and create value? (innovation and learning perspective)

- How do we look to our shareholders? (financial perspective)

Exhibit 2-1 indicates the linkages between the four perspectives. The advantage of the balanced scorecard over traditional measures is that three of the four perspectives (customer, innovation, and internal) are more than results—they are levers that managers can use to improve future results. The disadvantage is that scorecard measures are not public, which makes comparisons between competing enterprises impossible. Nor do the scorecards aid our analysis of year-over-year trends in specific areas of enterprise activity, such as inventory turnover and solvency. Used together, however, the balanced scorecard and traditional ratio analysis can help managers understand *and* improve their operations.

Summing Up

Financial statements tell a story about a company's strengths and weaknesses, and about various aspects of performance. But the story doesn't jump off the page—you have to dig, compare, and analyze to understand it. This chapter has shown how you can use ratios and percentage-format statements to understand the story on company profitability, key operating activities, solvency, and debt structure. In particular, it looked at three ratios:

- Profitability ratios, which associate the amount of income earned with the resources used. The ratios include return on assets (ROA), return on equity (ROE), and earnings per share (EPS).

- Activity ratios, which indicate how well assets were utilized. Days of receivables outstanding and inventory turnover are activity ratios.

- Solvency ratios, which indicate the ability of an organization to meet its financial obligations. These ratios include the current ratio, acid-test ratio, debt ratio, debt-to-equity ratio, and times interest earned ratio.

FIGURE 2-1

The Balanced Scorecard Links Performance Measures

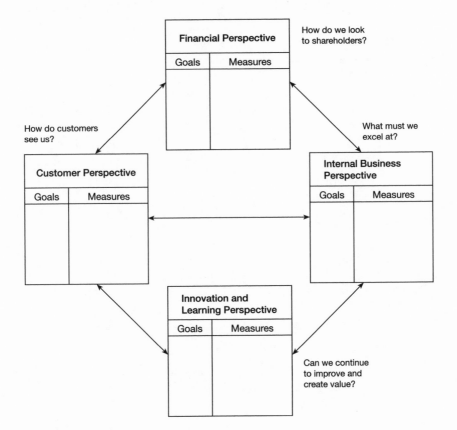

Source: Robert S. Kaplan and David P. Norton, "The Balanced Scorecard," *Harvard Business Review* 70, no. 1 (January–February 1992): 72.

Unfortunately, financial statements represent the past and are strictly limited to financial measurements. As a manager, you need leading indicators and nonfinancial measurements to understand and guide your business. This chapter has provided an introduction to the balanced scorecard, which many companies have adopted to complement their financial measures. To learn more about the balanced scorecard, see the For Further Reading section at the end of this book.

3

Important Accounting Concepts

The Rules That Shape Financial Statements

Key Topics Covered in This Chapter

- *Generally accepted accounting principles*

- *Accrual versus cash accounting*

- *Accounting for inventories*

- *Depreciation and its several methods*

- *Capitalizing leases*

- *The principle of historical cost and its implications*

- *Cost accounting and its uses*

CHAPTERS 1 AND 2 EXPLAINED the financial statements used by businesses and how you can use them to assess managerial performance and financial soundness. Mastery of these will help you at many points in your business career. As a consumer of financial information, you will also benefit from understanding some important accounting concepts that shape financial statements, particularly the ones covered here.

Generally Accepted Accounting Principles

It is important to understand that the values represented in financial statements are drawn from the business's accounting system. That system is designed to record, classify, and report the business's many monetary transactions in ways that conform with *generally accepted accounting principles,* or GAAP.

In the United States, GAAP is a body of conventions, rules, and procedures sanctioned by the Financial Accounting Standards Board, an independent, self-regulating body. All entities must follow GAAP in accounting for transactions and in representing their results in financial statements. This conformity to uniform standards gives shareholders, investors, lenders, customers, and regulators some assurance that the financial statements they see are accurate and fair representations of underlying business activities. As a check against manipulation, the financial statements of every corporation whose stock is publicly traded in the United States must be audited by an independent certified public accountant. This auditor examines the accounting records of the company and then renders an opinion as to the fairness and consistency of the company's financial statements and its conformity to GAAP.

An audit is designed to provide "reasonable" assurance that the financial statements are a fair representation of a company's financial transactions. It is not, however, an absolute assurance, since the auditor examines evidence on a test basis using statistical sampling. The auditor does not examine every transaction and amount. Some portions of a company's annual report—for example, the chairman's letter to shareholders, management's discussion and analysis of results, and information about stock prices—are not audited at all.

Accrual versus Cash Accounting

Businesses can use either *cash-basis accounting* or *accrual accounting*. But once they make the choice, they must adhere to it consistently.

Cash-basis accounting records transactions when cash has traded hands. Many small businesses use this method because it is simple and gives the proprietor some flexibility in "managing" taxable income.

In contrast to cash-basis accounting, accrual accounting records transactions as they are made, whether or not cash has actually changed hands. Most companies of any size use accrual accounting. This system provides a better matching between revenues and their associated cost, which helps companies understand the true causes and effects of business activities. Accordingly, revenues are recognized during the period in which the sales activities occur, whereas expenses are recognized in the same period as their associated revenues.

Note that in this example, Amalgamated could record $20,000 in revenues from hat rack orders in one tax year, even though payment for the orders might not be received until the next tax year. Also, recognition of the expenses for the materials associated with those orders is made as the order transactions are made.

Case Study: Cash-Basis Accounting for When Cash Trades Hands

Leo is a freelance writer who uses cash-basis accounting in his business. He has had a very lucrative year so far and is concerned about all the income tax he will have to pay if he is pushed into a higher tax bracket. But he knows that he has two ways of reducing his taxable income for this particular year: (1) defer the cash receipt of income from his clients until the next tax year, and (2) increase his tax-deductible cash expenses in this tax year.

So, as December rolls around, Leo decides to delay the billing of two clients until late in the month. That way, he'll receive the income in mid-January of the *next* tax year. He also thinks about all the business-related items he planned on purchasing over the upcoming months: stamps, a new computer, office supplies, reference materials, and so forth. And he makes those purchases before December 31. These go onto his books as cash expenses in that year—further reducing his taxable income.

Another interesting effect of accrual accounting is the treatment of so-called prepaid expenses. Some companies purchase multiyear leases and insurance policies with a single payment. These represent prepaid expenses. When initially made, they are recorded on the balance sheet as, for example, prepaid insurance. Each year's portion of that payment is charged off as an expense as it is used. For example, if Amalgamated purchased a two-year property insurance policy for $6,000 in 2002, $3,000 would be charged off as an expense on its year 2002 income statement and the advanced payment for 2003 would be carried as a prepaid asset on its balance sheet.

Accounting for Inventory

Inventory describes inputs to the production process: the supplies, raw materials, components, and so forth, that a company uses in its

Case Study: Accrual Accounting Matches Expenses to Activity

At Amalgamated Hat Rack, which manufactures hat racks from imitation moose antlers, the revenue for a customer order is booked as each hat rack is shipped—even if payment isn't made immediately. Similarly, if Amalgamated receives two thousand brass hooks from a contracted supply company, those hooks are not all expensed at once. Rather, they are expensed on a per-unit basis: If it takes five brass hooks to make one hat rack, then the brass hooks are expensed five at a time as each hat rack is shipped out.

operations. The term also includes work in process—goods in various stages of production—as well as finished goods waiting to be sold and/or shipped.

Inventories are a significant current asset for many firms. Accounting for them has two important aspects. First, the cost of inventory that is purchased or manufactured has to be determined. That cost is then held in the company's inventory accounts until the product is sold. Once the product has been shipped or delivered to a customer, the cost becomes an expense that is reported on the income statement as part of the cost of goods sold.

To understand the process of inventory accounting, imagine costs flowing into the inventory account and then being removed from that same account and charged to the cost of goods sold in the income statement. Just as products are physically moved into a warehouse and then physically removed as they are delivered to customers, the cost of inventory is moved into an account and later removed from it. It is important to recognize, however, that these flows need not be parallel—that is, the flow of costs into, and out of, the inventory account need not be in the same order as the flow of goods into, and out of, the warehouse. As will be explained later, we might decide to first use the inventory items most recently received because they will give us a more realistic estimate of our costs.

Inventory Cost Flows

At first glance, you may see no need to make an assumption about how costs flow through the inventory account. The cost of each item placed in the physical inventory can be entered into the account, and then, as the item is physically taken from inventory, the cost can be removed from the account. In this way, the costs accumulated in the account can perfectly match the items physically held, and the costs of goods sold can equal the sum of the cost of each item actually delivered to a customer. Such an inventory cost system can be identified as a specific identification system.[1]

Specifically identifying each item in inventory is relatively easy if each item is unique, such as an art object or a piece of custom-made furniture, or if each item has an identification number, such as an automobile. However, specific identification is not practical when inventory items are not individually identifiable. This is the case with bushels of wheat, caseloads of memory chips, and loads of brass hooks like the ones used in Amalgamated's hat racks. In these cases, accountants commonly assume a flow of cost through the inventory account that is not necessarily related to the actual physical flow of goods.

The accounting problem with these all-the-same inventory items is complicated by the company's possibly having paid different prices for them. For example, Amalgamated has 5,000 brass hooks in its parts inventory. Because of inflation and other factors, the company paid $0.10 for 1,500 hooks; $0.12 for 2,000; and the bargain price of $0.08 for the remaining 1,500. So when its assembly crews pull 200 hooks from inventory, which cost should be reflected in the cost of goods sold? The hooks are identical in every sense except their order of purchase and their cost to Amalgamated.

Three common assumptions are used in accounting for inventory cost: *average cost, first-in, first-out* (FIFO), and *last-in, first-out* (LIFO). A company can choose any of these three assumptions and use them consistently for each classification of inventory, regardless of how the goods physically move into and out of inventory.

Using the average-cost method requires you to calculate the average cost of items in the beginning inventory plus the purchases made during the accounting period to determine the cost of goods sold and the cost of inventory on hand at the end of the period. The average cost is assumed to be a representative cost of all the items available for sale during the accounting period. Rather than wait until the end of an accounting period to calculate the average cost, some companies use a predetermined unit cost of all transactions that take place during the accounting period. This is a standard-cost system and is a variation of the average-cost method. Any difference between the actual average unit cost and the predetermined standard cost during a period is usually added to or subtracted from the cost of goods sold for that period.

If the first-in, first-out, or FIFO, assumption is used, then the oldest costs in the inventory account are the first to be transferred to the cost of goods sold when merchandise is sold. Using this assumption means that the costs retained in the inventory account will always be those most recently incurred for the purchase or manufacture of inventory. For this reason, the FIFO assumption produces an inventory account balance that usually comes the closest of the three methods to approximating the replacement cost of the inventory.

The last-in, first-out, or LIFO, assumption is the opposite of FIFO. The cost of goods sold is measured using the cost of the *most recent* additions to inventory, and the inventory account always retains the most distant items purchased or manufactured. This assumed inventory consumption pattern may be quite different from the actual physical flow of goods, and the pattern usually is different when the LIFO method is used. If older costs are retained in the inventory account for some period because the inventory is never depleted, and if prices change substantially in the same period, the LIFO inventory balance will likely bear little relation to the current value of the same amount of inventory recently purchased.

Use of the LIFO assumption is not permitted in some countries. It is, however, permitted in the United States and is quite popular there. One important reason for this popularity is that LIFO provides a better measure of the current costs of inventory. When those costs are matched against current sales revenues, both investors and managers get a better sense of what's going on in the business. Another reason for LIFO's popularity is that inflation generally makes the most currently acquired inventory more expensive. This increased cost reduces the reported profitability of sales, which, in turn, reduces the tax liability.

To get a better idea of how the three common assumptions—average cost, LIFO, and FIFO—affect the cost of goods sold, consider this example. Amalgamated Hat Rack maintained an inventory of brass fixtures for use in its deluxe, limited-edition hat rack assemblies. In 2002, owing to increasing copper prices, the price paid to suppliers for these fixtures increased significantly. A record of purchases in 2002 showed the following:

February 1	50 at $6.00	$300
April 1	50 at $7.50	$375
May 1	50 at $8.50	$425
July 1	50 at $9.00	$450
October 1	50 at $10.50	$525
Total		$2,075

Price had been stable before 2002. On January 1, 2002, there were twenty-nine fixtures on hand, each of which had cost $5.00. At the end of the year, there were fifty-four on hand.

It's the Law

For most accounting methods, U.S. tax law has no requirement that the same method be employed in financial reports issued to shareholders and in financial reports on which taxes are based. However, LIFO is an exception. A company that chooses to save taxes by using the LIFO assumption must also use the LIFO method in its reports to shareholders. For this reason, there is a downside associated with paying lower taxes: Management must then report to shareholders lower earnings than might be the case if an alternative inventory assumption were used.

If inventories are valued periodically, the value of inventory in terms of historical prices and the cost of fixtures sold depends on the inventory flow assumption adopted (table 3-1). Notice that in the calculation of LIFO, average cost, and FIFO, we calculate the cost of fixtures sold by starting with the cost of the fixtures available for use ($2,220 in each case). We reduce that figure by the cost of the fifty-four units available at year's end under each assumption. In the LIFO calculation, for example, the cost of the remaining fifty-four is assumed to be the cost of the first (and lowest-cost) fixtures purchased.

For managers, the important thing to remember is that the inventory-cost-flow assumption has an impact on the cost of goods sold, the reported net income, and the inventory value that will be shown among the current assets on the balance sheet. What's more, if

TABLE 3-1

Amalgamated Hat Rack, Value of Inventory, 2002

	INVENTORY-FLOW ASSUMPTION		
	FIFO Method	Average-Cost Method	LIFO Method
Fixtures, Jan. 1, 2002 (29 at $5.00)	$145	$145	$145
Purchases, 2002	$2,075	$2,075	$2,075
Available for Use, 2002	$2,220	$2,220	$2,220
Fixtures on Hand, 12/31/2002	$561[a]	$430[b]	$295[c]
Cost of Fixtures Sold, 2002	$1,659	$1,790	$1,925

Source: Adapted from William J. Bruns, Jr., "Accounting for Current Assets," Case 193-048 (Boston: Harvard Business School Publishing, revised August 13,1996).

[a]FIFO method: The total cost of 50 fixtures at $10.50 (or $525) plus 4 fixtures at $9.00 ($36).

[b]Average-cost method: The total cost of 54 fixtures at the average cost of $7.96, calculated by taking the total cost of brass fixtures purchased and dividing by the total number of fixtures used in production.

[c]LIFO method: The total cost of 29 fixtures at $5.00 ($145) plus 25 fixtures at $6.00 ($150).

the costs of inventory have risen and the LIFO method is utilized, then dipping into old inventory costs by reducing the size of the inventory on hand (called a LIFO liquidation) will give a burst of net income, which may not be sustainable in future periods.

We can sum up our discussion of inventory accounting quite simply. Inventory accounting consists of two steps: First, you must measure the cost of items added to inventory. Second, you must decide which method you will use to account for the cost of these items as they are sold or delivered to customers.

Depreciation

Expenditures for property and capital equipment represent a commitment of resources to assets ordinarily utilized over several periods. The accounting concept of matching revenues with their related expenses requires that the cost of such investments be matched with the revenues obtained from using them. For buildings and equipment, the amount of expense matched with revenues is called *depreciation*. Depreciation is a noncash expense that effectively reduces the balance-sheet value of an asset over its presumed useful life. For example, if Amalgamated were to purchase for $50,000 (delivered and installed) a new piece of metal-bending machinery that had an anticipated useful life of twenty years, then the company could expense a portion of that $50,000 against revenues in each of the following twenty years. This would reduce the company's taxable income dollar for dollar. At the same time, Amalgamated's accountants would reduce the balance-sheet value of the machinery at the same rate until the value was zero.[2]

The term "noncash expense" is worth remembering. Even though depreciation is listed as an expense on the income statement, no money flows out of the company's pockets—unlike expenses such as salaries, supplies, utilities, and postage. Depreciation is simply a handy (though imperfect) way of recognizing that certain assets wear out or gradually lose their productive value and must be replaced.

If the asset is a natural resource, such as forest land or mineral deposits, similar expenses would be called depletion. If the asset is intangible (e.g., a patent), its original cost would be amortized over the periods when benefits are obtained or, in some cases, over an arbitrary period.

Understanding this simple explanation of depreciation is bound to help you as a manager. A knowledge of other, more detailed aspects of depreciation will help you even more. Let's look at some of them.

The Cost of Fixed Assets

The cost of a fixed asset and the amount at which it will be initially carried in reports consist of the total amount of expenditures necessary to ready the asset for its intended use. This means that in addition to the price of acquiring legal title to an asset, you must add the costs of delivery, installation, employee training, and the modification of facilities necessary to use the asset as planned.

Estimating Depreciation

At the beginning of the life of an asset, an estimate of the asset's salvage value is made. The salvage value is the expected selling price of the asset less any removal costs at the end of its useful life to the organization. The difference between the cost and the salvage value is called the depreciable cost. It is this depreciable cost that is to be matched in some way to revenues earned in the accounting periods over which the asset will be used. Here's an example, using a laboratory furnace that Amalgamated Hat Racks acquired to develop new alloys for the metal fixtures on its new high-performance hat racks.

Price of furnace	$13,000
Less: discount for paying cash	$500
Price paid	$12,500
Freight charges	$500
Installation	$2,000

Training expenses	<u>$1,000</u>
Total cost	$16,000
Less: salvage value	<u>$6,000</u>
Depreciable cost	$10,000

Once we have determined the depreciable cost, all that remains is to select a method for allocating that cost to periods when the asset will be used to generate revenues. In allocating the depreciable cost, any one of several methods is acceptable. Although these methods may appear arbitrary, they meet two criteria. First, the amount of depreciation charged is not subject to manipulation by management in such a way that the company's income for any period can be capriciously distorted. Second, the amounts charged bear some resemblance to the decline in value of the asset measured on a historical cost basis.

We will look at two methods of depreciation in common use with occasional variations in each: straight-line depreciation and declining-balance depreciation. Each method has its advantages.

Straight-Line Depreciation

Under the straight-line method of estimating depreciation, an equal portion of the depreciable cost is charged each year according to some measure of the length of an asset's life. Under this method, as under any method of depreciation commonly used, the amount charged to expense is usually accumulated and shown on the balance sheet as a deduction from the historical cost of the asset. This accumulated depreciation is called a contra asset. It is always associated with the asset to which it is related, and its balance offsets part of the original cost that has already been matched against revenues. Table 3-2 shows how depreciation for Amalgamated's new furnace can be estimated with the straight-line method. The method employs an estimated useful life of five years and, alternatively, the furnace's anticipated lifetime metal-melting capacity and the company's production outlook.

TABLE 3-2

Straight-Line Depreciation for Laboratory Furnace

DEPRECIABLE COST:

Price of Furnace	$13,000
Less: Discount	500
	$12,500
Freight Charge	500
Installation	2,000
Training Expenses	1,000
Total Cost	$16,000
Less: Salvage Value	6,000
Depreciable Cost	$10,000

Estimated life: 5 years
Expected metal melt: 250,000 pounds

SCHEDULE OF DEPRECIATION EXPENSE:

Year	Expected Melt (in Pounds)	Time Base	Use Base
1	40,000	$2,000	$1,600
2	45,000	2,000	1,800
3	50,000	2,000	2,000
4	55,000	2,000	2,200
5	60,000	2,000	2,400
Total	250,000	$10,000	$10,000

Source: William J. Bruns, Jr., "Accounting for Property, Plant, Equipment and Other Assets," Case 9-193-046 (Boston: Harvard Business School, revised August 13, 1996).

Declining–Balance Depreciation

In an attempt to reflect that an asset is often most productive in the early years of its use, accountants often employ methods that charge a larger proportion of the total depreciation expense in the early years of life than they do in later periods. One common method for accomplishing this is to charge to each period a fixed percentage of the original cost of the asset less any previously accumulated depreciation. (Note the difference from straight-line depreciation, in which the depreciation rate is applied to the entire depreciable cost of the asset each period.) Commonly, this figure will be 150 or 200 percent of the depreciation rate used under the straight-line method. Because the declining-balance method will never completely amortize the original cost of an asset, accountants typically do not deduct the salvage value of the asset from the original cost before applying the depreciation percentage.

Table 3–3 shows how Amalgamated's accountants would use the declining–balance method to calculate the depreciation of its laboratory furnace. Again, this example adhered to a five-year depreciation period. However, since the $6,000 salvage value is not excluded in this method, the depreciable cost of the furnace is $16,000.

One very nice advantage of this declining-balance method is the much larger depreciation expenses allowed in the early years. This means that Amalgamated can make much larger reductions in its taxable income in the earlier years. And as you may already know, a dollar of taxes that you can defer until later is a dollar you can use to invest in money–making operations today.

Final Comments about Depreciation

The importance of depreciation lies in its relationship to the proper determination of income. But which method is best? Ideally, the best method should provide the best estimation of real profit. In practice, however, other criteria often dominate: simplicity of application, tax and other legal requirements, or the desire on the part of management to show earnings more favorable or less favorable than

TABLE 3-3

Declining Balance Depreciation

Year	Book Value at Beginning of Year	Depreciation Expense (40 Percent of Book Value)	Book Value at End of Year
1	$16,000	$6,400	$9,600
2	9,600	3,840	5,760
3	5,760	2,304	3,456
4	3,456	1,382	2,074
5	2,074	<u>829</u>	1,245
Total		<u>$14,755</u>	

Source: William J. Bruns, Jr., "Accounting for Property, Plant, Equipment and Other Assets," Case 9-193-046 (Boston: Harvard Business School, revised August 13, 1996).

those with another method. Estimates of depreciation expense, therefore, must be used and interpreted with great care.

Another aspect of depreciation accounting deserves mention. We have dealt with the depreciation of individual assets because this was the easiest way to illustrate different methods of depreciation. In practice, however, a large firm may have many assets of a certain type—personal computers, for example. Rather than keep track of each asset, accountants find it more feasible to depreciate them as a group.

Accounting for Leases

You probably know about leasing a new automobile. The ads are enticing. "Drive away in a new MegaGuzzler SUV for only $299 per month!" Then the fine print tells you about the four-year term of the lease and the $2,500 or so you must pay up front to get that low monthly lease rate.

Car leases are convenient when you don't want to take out a loan. And sometimes, you don't even have to make a down payment (though your monthly payments will be higher). At the end of the multiyear lease term, you can return the car and walk away. For some people, this is a good alternative to owning a car.

Companies like leases for some of the same reasons. Leasing, in fact, is an extremely popular approach to acquiring assets, and everything from computers to railroad cars to skyscrapers can be leased today. Organizations that lease assets rather than purchase them may do so for various reasons. Through leasing, a company can enjoy the use of certain resources without paying for them until it can obtain receipts from customers. This frees the firm from the necessity of borrowing and thus depleting liquid assets. Likewise, companies that find themselves short on cash and long on fixed assets often sell their assets. Then, with the next stroke of the pen, the companies lease them back from the buyer—an arrangement known as a *sale and leaseback*. More than a few grandiose corporate headquarters buildings have gone though this transaction, usually when the selling corporation has fallen on hard times.

As a manager, you should understand a few aspects of this form of financing and its accounting requirements. First, leasing agreements fall into two main classes. An *operating lease* is the most familiar. The personal automobile lease usually falls into this class. In this lease, the term only covers a portion of the asset's anticipated useful life. The lessor (the asset's owner) must renew the lease one or more times to recoup the cost of the asset and make a profit.

A *financial lease,* in contrast, typically covers the entire useful life of the asset. And the lease cannot be canceled unless the lessee makes all the scheduled payments. Also, the lessee typically must pay the taxes, insurance, and maintenance costs related to the asset. This is very much like purchasing the asset and making monthly payments until the asset is completely paid for. Since the lease agreement requires the outflow of cash in the future, it has the essential characteristics of a liability.

Years ago, leases were a convenient source of off-balance-sheet financing for corporations. Companies could obligate themselves in a financial lease—just as they would if they had used a loan to purchase an asset—but they would not have to list the asset and its corresponding liability on the balance sheet. (The inclusion of the lease on the balance sheet is called capitalizing the lease.) This practice made these companies' debt-to-interest ratios appear healthier than they truly were. The situation changed in 1976, when the Financial Accounting Standards Board required corporations to capitalize their leases on the balance sheet when those leases were, in reality, purchase and loan agreements under another name. Operating leases, however, need only be shown in the footnotes of corporate financial statements.

For example, consider a company that, needing cash for other investments, has sold its sole building and leased it back in a financial lease. Table 3-4 shows the balance sheets of the company before and after it leased its building. For simplicity, we assume that the company sells the building at its balance-sheet value. Prior to the sale-and-leaseback arrangement, this company had only one asset—its building—and no liabilities.

The sale converts the building asset into another asset: cash, which the company can use to finance potential money-making

TABLE 3-4

Assets and Liabilities of a Hypothetical Company Before and After Leasing Its Building

	Before Leasing	After Leasing
Assets		
Building	$50,000	$0
Cash	$0	$50,000
Capitalized Lease	_____	$50,000
Total Assets	$50,000	$100,000
Liabilities		
Liabilities	$0	$50,000
Owners' Equity	$50,000	$50,000
Total Liabilities and Owners' Equity	$50,000	$100,000

activities. But since this is a financial lease, GAAP requires the company to capitalize the lease and show it as a liability on its balance sheet. Notice that owners' equity remains the same despite the accounting sleight of hand.

Historic Cost and Its Implications

For the many balance-sheet assets discussed in chapter 1—cash, inventories, property, and equipment—GAAP has a strict rule: They must be recorded at their historic cost. Thus, the land and building that your employer acquired in 1946 for its headquarters in midtown Manhattan at a cost of $300,000 must be represented today at that figure less depreciation. No matter that the property is now worth $10 gazillion—it goes on the books at its acquisition cost.

Real property isn't the only category of assets whose real value may be less than its balance-sheet value. Consider inventory. It follows the same rule. Thus, if the publisher of Paul Samuelson's famous textbook on economics were to come out in a new edition, the market value of the inventory of the previous edition would fall like a stone, since just about everyone would want the new edition. The listed balance-sheet value of the previous edition's inventory, however, would remain the same—at its historic cost. (Some companies include an inventory value reserve to reflect the lost value that some percentage of inventory will likely incur.)

The historic-cost principle obviously results in a disparity between real and accounting-statement values. So why do accountants adhere to it? The reason is that they have found no better alternative. Obviously, companies cannot be trusted to write the values up or down on their own. And it would be hugely expensive and impractical to have all corporate assets valued by an army of independent appraisers every year. So we are stuck with the system we have. Your best defense against misinterpreting balance-sheet values is your knowledge that they are recorded at their historic cost.

Cost Accounting

Cost accounting is a branch of accounting that keeps track of the cost of the many things that go directly or indirectly into the production of each unit of goods and services sold by the company. Managers can use this information for several purposes:

- To develop reasonable selling prices for the goods and services they produce

- To identify costs that are getting out of control

- To target particular costs for gradual reduction

- To determine which products and services are profitable and which are not

Some costs are *direct,* and others are *indirect.* Cost accountants are interested in both, and managers should be as well. For Amalgamated Hat Rack, for example, screws, glue, lumber, purchased brass fixtures, and labor are all direct costs of producing the company's products. Indirect costs, often called *overhead, allocations,* or *burden,* are costs that cannot be attributed to the production of any particular unit of output—the rent on the production facility, utilities costs, the salaries and benefits of executives and administrative personnel, property taxes, and the cost of the annual company picnic, for example. In most cases, these overhead costs are allocated to units of production according to some formula.

For example, Amalgamated Hat Rack's cost accountants keep track of every little thing that goes into the cost of producing the Model 1 hat rack, a key product line. They account for the costs of machine hours, labor hours, materials, per-unit shipping—even the commissions paid to its independent sales reps. These direct costs amount to $26. In the parlance of accounting, we say that any amount the company gets for a Model 1 hat rack above that figure represents its *contribution margin,* or its contribution to overhead and profits. More specifically, the contribution margin per unit is defined as follows:

Contribution Margin = Net Revenue − Direct Costs

For example, if the Model 1 sold for $50 per unit, then each unit sold would contribute $24 ($50, less $26 in direct costs) to overhead and profits.

Now let's look at the total direct and indirect costs of producing the Model 1:

Pine lumber	$1.55
Purchased brass hardware	$2.50
Glue	$0.05
Machine time	$0.60
Labor (0.75 hours at $20 per hour)	$15.00
Shipping (average)	$3.30
Commission	$3.00
Total direct cost	$26.00
Overhead charge	$17.55
Total direct and indirect cost	$43.55

Note that Amalgamated's cost accountants have tacked on $17.55 in overhead for each Model 1. Assuming that the company's cost information is complete and accurate, this means that each sale of a Model 1 contributes $6.45 to profits ($50, less $26 direct cost, less $17.55 in overhead charges).

Process versus Job–Order Costing

Accountants generally use one of two very different costing systems, depending on the nature of the business: process costing, or job-order costing. Process costing works well when a company mass-produces thousands of identical items, such as screws, memory chips, or light bulbs. This cost system focuses on the costs of the several steps of the process—for example, blending, extruding, cutting, and packaging. The raw materials and the cost of each step are calculated and then divided by the number of units churned out.

Job-order costing is more appropriate for custom manufacturing. For example, a builder of made-to-order machine tools or a lunar lander would use this approach. Job order costing identifies all costs relevant to the particular job, direct and indirect.

Using Cost Information

Managers use cost information to understand and control the variables that determine profitability. For instance, most manufacturing companies determine a standard cost for each direct-cost item, such as labor cost per unit, machine hours per unit, and lumber cost per unit. The accounting department then produces a monthly statement that indicates the actual cost for each. Managers can then easily see the variances between standard and actual and can investigate the causes if those variances are getting out of hand. They can also identify the major contributors to cost and work to reign them in. Amalgamated's managers, for example, can see that labor is a major contributor to the cost of producing Model 1 hat racks. This information should spur them to reexamine production itself to see if they can alter the process to produce the same number of units with fewer labor hours. Alternatively, management could investigate any production equipment that might substitute for labor and at a lower per-unit cost.

Activity-Based Costing

Overhead, or indirect cost, has been the weak point in many cost accounting systems. Traditionally, accountants used simple formulas to allocate indirect costs. For instance, many allocated the total of indirect costs among products according to the number of labor hours attributed to each product. This was a reasonable approach as long as labor was the biggest cost of production. Other approaches divided up indirect costs in proportion to the revenues realized from each product. This, too, often made sense, as long as the products weren't too different.

Today, however, labor is rarely the major cost factor, and most factories are capable of producing dozens or hundreds of different kinds of products. As a result, the old allocation formulas no longer produce good approximations of indirect costs. In fact, those formulas can easily lead managers to step up production of money-losing products and drop their most profitable product lines. To understand how this mismatch of real and apparent profitability occurs, consider what would happen to a company that traditionally relied on labor hours as the formula for allocating overhead. In the days when labor was a major cost of production, this would put a major proportion of total overhead on the backs of company products that used lots of labor—which made sense. However, as some lines of products modernized and eliminated labor through automation, their share of the overhead burden would shrink. And the profitability of these products would appear to grow. But overhead costs would not go away; they would simply be shifted elsewhere.

Thus, other product lines—particularly those that used high inputs of labor—would have to absorb the lion's share of company-wide overhead. This would make their products appear relatively unprofitable. To see how this could happen, consider two products, both of which net the same revenue per unit ($14.00) and which have the same direct cost of manufacture, shipping, and distribution ($5.00). Product A has the same contribution margin as does product B. Product A enjoys market leadership and growing demand. But because its manufacture involves more labor hours, the company's cost formula has allocated a much higher overhead charge to it—so much so that product A is shown to produce a $1.00 loss per unit sale. Product B, in comparison, is a weak performer in a declining market. Yet because of its low labor content, it receives a much lower overhead allocation, which makes it appear very profitable. Seeing these numbers, management could easily make an entirely wrong-headed decision: Phase out production of product A, and increase production of product B. Decisions like these can sink even the best companies!

	Product A	Product B
Total direct cost	$5.00	$5.00
Overhead charge	$10.00	$4.00
Total direct/indirect	$15.00	$9.00

Net revenue/unit	$14.00	$14.00
Contribution to profits	$(1.00)	$5.00

H. Thomas Johnson and Robert Kaplan proposed an alternative way of figuring costs.[3] That alternative came to be known as *activity-based costing,* or ABC. ABC is an approach to cost accounting that carefully quantifies the links between performing particular activities and the demands those activities make on the organization's resources. While traditional cost-accounting systems allocate indirect and support costs to products through such measures as direct labor hours, machine hours, or materials cost, ABC recognizes that different products, customers, brands, and distribution channels make very different demands on a company's resources. Accordingly, ABC starts by creating a hierarchy of activities and then assigns costs according to the activity involved. It counts the actual activities that go into making a specific product (or into delivering a specific service) and attempts to figure the costs of those activities. Rather than allocate the total cost of a machine across a range of products according to a formula, for example, ABC-trained accountants study how much machine time (including setup, etc.) each product actually requires, then allocate costs accordingly. ABC also focuses on cost drivers that can guide allocations. The cost of the human resources department, for instance, might be assessed among units according to each unit's head count.

ABC has spread rapidly, though not as rapidly as its proponents had hoped. One reason for the hesitation is that it involves a trade-off: For the sake of more accuracy, a company must spend more time and resources counting and measuring the activities that drive costs. A company must expect a clear benefit from embracing the idea—and even if there is such a benefit, will it be large enough to justify reprogramming the necessary systems?

Summing Up

There's a lot more to accounting than what we've discussed in these pages, but the following topics covered here will help you make sense of many important accounting issues that affect your performance as a manager:

- Generally accepted accounting principles, or GAAP

- Accrual versus cash accounting

- Accounting for inventories

- Accounting for depreciation

- The account treatment of leases

- The principle of historic cost

- Cost accounting

Of these accounting issues, cost accounting is one that the manager not directly involved in finance is most likely to encounter on a regular basis. It can help you understand which of your operations or products are economically contributing to profits and which are not. Cost accounting can also help you avoid arbitrary assignments of overhead that make valid profitability assessment impossible. For further information on cost accounting and the other topics covered in this chapter, please refer to the sources listed under the For Further Reading section at the end of this book.

4

Taxes

Important Details You Should Know

Key Topics Covered in This Chapter

- *Taxes for different legal forms of business*

- *Progressive tax rates*

- *Marginal rate*

- *Tax credits versus tax deductions*

- *Tax loss carrybacks and carryforwards*

INCOME TAXES in the United States are a big, complex subject. Congress has made them that way. When federal income taxes were first instituted in 1913 under the provisions of the sixteenth amendment to the U.S. Constitution, the tax return consisted of only one page, and the entire tax code filled less than fourteen pages. Today, at over twenty thousand pages, the U.S. tax code is the product of years of incremental additions, tinkering, and special exceptions for certain companies and industries. And Congress hasn't finished yet. Every year, hundreds of pages are added to the code, prompting one critic to complain that the system is like an old, leaky tire with thousands of patches.

The code is so arcane that all sizable businesses and many private citizens rely on tax professionals to steer them clear of its many shoals. Even tax professionals cannot fathom the entire code. Instead they specialize in one or two of its aspects: estate taxes, qualified retirement plans, real estate taxes, corporate taxes for extraction industries, and so forth.

As bad as this may seem, there is a silver lining for the business manager who does not specialize in finance: Your company assigns its tax issues to specialists, leaving you off the hook. Nevertheless, it pays to understand some basic tax concepts, since taxes creep into most financial decisions. This advice is doubly true for business owners.

Since business taxes are too big a subject to tackle in a single chapter—let alone in a single book—this chapter will confine itself to just a few things you ought to understand. We'll start with how the different legal forms of business are taxed in the United States. We'll then move on to two related subjects: progressive tax rates and the concept of marginal rate. These set up the next section, in which the differences between tax deductions and tax credits are explained. We'll end with the subject of tax loss carryback and carryforward.

Taxes and the Legal Form of the Business

One of the key issues that every entrepreneur must address at the onset of a new venture is the legal form the enterprise should adopt. This decision is driven chiefly by the objectives of the entrepreneur and the firm's investors. But taxation and legal liabilities also play a part. The choice is made difficult by the trade-offs built into the law. To get the most favorable tax treatment, a business must often give up some protection from liability, some flexibility, or both.[1]

Sole Proprietorships

The *sole proprietorship* is the oldest, simplest, and most common form of business entity. It is a business owned by a single individual. This owner and the business are one and the same for tax and legal liability purposes. The proprietorship is not taxed as a separate entity. Instead, the owner reports all income and deductible expenses for the business on Schedule C of his or her personal income tax return.

Note that the earnings of the business are taxed at the individual level, whether or not they are actually distributed in cash. There is no vehicle for sheltering income.

For liability purposes, the individual and the business are also one and the same. Thus, legal claimants can pursue the personal property of the proprietor, not simply the assets that are utilized in the business.

C Corporations

The C corporation is synonymous with the common notion of a corporation. When a business incorporates, it becomes a C corporation unless it makes a special election to become an S corporation, which will be described later.

C corporations in the United States are hugely outnumbered by sole proprietorships, yet they account for almost 90 percent of all U.S. sales. This economic dominance by corporations stems from the adoption of the corporate form by most of the nation's largest enterprises. The corporate form is appealing for several reasons. First, in contrast to the sole proprietorship, the C corporation's owners are personally protected from liability. Consider the case of the massive oil spill of the oil tanker *Exxon Valdez*. Even if the damages against Exxon had bankrupted the company, the courts could not have pursued the individual shareholders for further damages. An individual owner's liability is limited to the extent of his or her investment in the firm. This corporate shell, or veil, can only be pierced in the event of fraud.

In exchange for limited liability, the C corporation is considered a tax-paying entity. Because dividends paid out to shareholders are not deductible from corporate income, the earnings of a corporation are taxed twice.

The C corporation does, however, enjoy certain tax benefits that other forms of businesses do not share, or do not share to the same

Case Study: Double Jeopardy of C Corporations

Amalgamated Hat Rack earned $647,500 before taxes and paid a little more than 46 percent of this ($300,000) in state and federal corporate income taxes, leaving it with $347,500 in profit after tax. If the company paid $10,000 of that in the form of a dividend to its founder and CEO, Angus McDuff, McDuff would be required to add that amount to his personal income, which might be taxed at about the same rate (state and federal). Thus, the same income is taxed twice. (Note: There is a minor exception to this double-taxation issue in the case of corporations that receive dividend income from other corporations.)

Case Study: Partnership Profit Is Personal

Bill and Bob formed a partnership and started a restaurant called The Billy-Bob Café. By agreement, they split the profits of the business equally, the total of which amounted to $140,000 last year. Bill, who had no other source earnings that year, reported $70,000 in income on his personal tax return. Bob, who earned another $20,000 from a part-time job, had to report $90,000 on his personal income tax return.

extent. The tax law affords favorable tax treatment for many fringe benefits provided by the corporation to its employees and owner/employees. For example, the corporation can deduct from its taxable income the death benefits it pays to the beneficiaries of deceased employees (up to a certain limit). It can set up 401(k) and other retirement plans with fairly generous tax-exempt annual contribution limits. It can also deduct its expense for employee health-care premiums.

Partnerships

A *partnership* is a business entity with two or more owners. It is treated like a proprietorship for tax and liability purposes. Earnings are distributed according to the partnership agreement and are treated as personal income for tax purposes. Thus, like the sole proprietorship, the partnership is simply a conduit for generating income for its partners.

Partnerships have a unique liability situation. Each partner is jointly and severally liable. Thus, a damaged party may pursue a single partner or any number of partners for any amount—the claim may not be proportional to the invested capital or the distribution of earnings.

A partnership involves complexities not faced by the sole proprietorship. The partners must resolve, and should set down in writing, their agreement on a number of issues:

- The amount and nature of their respective capital contributions (e.g., one partner might contribute cash, another a patent, and a third property and cash)

- The allocation of the business's profits and losses

- Salaries and drawings against profits

- Management responsibilities

- The consequences of withdrawal, retirement, disability, or the death of a partner

- The means of dissolution and liquidation of the partnership

Limited Partnerships

Limited partnerships are a hybrid form of organization having both limited and general partners. The general partner (and there may be more than one) assumes management responsibility and unlimited liability for the business and must have at least a 1 percent interest in profits and losses. The limited partner (or partners) has no voice in management and is legally liable only for the amount of his or her capital contribution plus any other debt obligations specifically accepted.

In a limited partnership, the general partner may be a corporation (i.e., a corporate general partner). When a corporation is the sole general partner, the corporation must have sufficient assets to cover the unlimited liability that it must assume. For this reason, the corporate general partner must have a net worth of at least $250,000, or 10 percent of the total capitalization of the partnership, whichever is less.

Note that in a limited partnership, profits and losses may be allocated differently among the partners. That is, even if profits are allocated 20 percent to the general partner and 80 percent to the limited partners, then the limited partners may get 99 percent of the losses. Losses, however, are deductible only up to the amount of capital at risk. The distribution of profit is subject to all sorts of creative structuring, such as those observed in certain venture capital and real estate partnerships. In some of those arrangements, the limited partners get 99 percent of the profits until they have gotten back an amount equal to their entire capital contributions, at which point the general partner gets 30 percent and the limited partners get only 70 percent.

S Corporations and Limited-Liability Companies

The S corporation is another creature of the tax law. It is a closely held corporation whose tax status is the same as the partnership's, but its participants enjoy the liability protections granted to corporate shareholders. In other words, it is a conduit for passing profits and losses directly to the personal income tax returns of its shareholders, whose legal liabilities are limited to the amount of their capital contributions. In exchange for these favorable treatments, the law places a number of restrictions on the types of corporations that can elect S status. To qualify for S corporation status, an organization must meet the following requirements:

- Have only one class of stock, although differences in voting rights are allowed

- Be a domestic corporation, owned wholly by U.S. citizens, and derive no more than 80 percent of its revenues from non-U.S. sources

- Have seventy-five or fewer stockholders (husbands and wives count as one stockholder)

- Derive no more than 25 percent of revenues from passive sources, such as interest, dividends, rents, and royalties

- Have only individuals, estates, and certain trusts as shareholders (i.e., no corporations or partnerships)

The last provision leaves out venture capitalists as potential shareholders since most venture-capitalist firms are partnerships.

The limited-liability company (LLC) is a relatively new type of entity designed to afford the same benefits as does the S corporation. The LLC is similar to an S corporation in that it enjoys the tax

advantages of a partnership and the liability protections of a corporation. Although state laws differ somewhat, an LLC is like an S corporation, but with none of the restrictions on the number or type of
shareholders. The LLC is similar to a partnership in that the LLC's
operating agreement (the equivalent of a partnership agreement)
may distribute profits and losses in a variety of ways, not necessarily
in proportion to capital contributions. Law firms are often organized
as LLCs. Table 4-1 summarizes the various legal forms of businesses
in the United States and their corresponding numbers.

Which Form Makes Sense?

As you have no doubt gathered, tax implications are an important
factor in the choice of a business entity. Indeed, the incentives of the
tax code give rise to certain tactics that can be risky. For instance, the
aforementioned double taxation of a corporation's distributed earnings provides an incentive for owner-employees to pay all profits
to themselves as compensation. Unlike dividends, compensation is
deductible as an expense to the corporation and is thus not taxed
twice. However, the Internal Revenue Service (IRS) has certain
rules on what is considered reasonable compensation; these rules are
designed to discourage just such behavior.

TABLE 4-1

Legal Forms of Businesses in the United States

	Number of Firms (Thousands)	Annual Receipts ($ Millions)
All Types	19,286	14,072
C Corporations	2,033	10,747
S Corporations	1,564	1,938
Partnerships	1,090	665
Individual Proprietorships	14,599	722

Source: U.S. Bureau of the Census, "Survey of Women-Owned Business"; and unpublished data.

Note too that the tax on individuals in so-called flow-through entities such as partnerships and LLCs is on the share of income *earned,* not on the actual cash *distributed.* The income of the partnership is taxed at the personal level of the partners, whether or not any cash is actually distributed.

If the venture is projected to create large losses in the early years, then there may be some benefit to passing those losses through to investors, assuming that the investors are in a position to use them to offset other income and thus reduce their taxes. This would favor the partnership or LLC. Similarly, if the business intends to generate substantial cash flow and return it to investors as the primary means of creating value for investors, then a partnership or LLC is still attractive. If however, the business will require cash investment over the long term, and value is intended to be harvested through a sale or public offering, then a C corporation is probably the most attractive option.

Of course, a business may move through many forms in its lifetime. A sole proprietorship may become a partnership and finally a C corporation. A limited partnership may become an LLC and then a C corporation. Each transition, however, will require considerable legal work and administrative burden for the management and owners of the firm. The advantages of the right form of organization at each particular stage certainly may warrant these burdens. On the other hand, high-potential ventures on the fast track do not want to lose time and focus by jumping through these legal hoops, especially when different modes of external financing must be addressed. Consequently, if you are an entrepreneur, consider the likely evolution of your business before selecting a particular form of organization, and consult with a qualified tax attorney or accountant before making this important choice.

Progressive Tax Rates

Tax rates for corporate and personal income are progressive. This means that the first bundle of taxable income is taxed at a low rate, whereas succeeding bundles are taxed at progressively higher rates. A cynic might say that a progressive tax rate is one that becomes progressively more painful. The U.S. federal taxes levied on corporations in 2001 are outlined in table 4-2.

As you can see, a corporation that reports taxable income of $50,000 or less pays at the 15 percent rate. But once it gets over $50,000, the rate jumps to 25 percent, and still higher as taxable income increases. The highest rate is on taxable incomes in the $100,001 through $334,999 range, which are tapped at a rate of 39 percent.

Oddly, the 2001 schedule of rates dips once a corporation hits the $335,000 mark and again at the $10 million mark, then continues to rise until taxable income hits $18.3 million, at which point the rate drops back again. One can only speculate about the reason for these bobbing rates. Volume discounts from the IRS? Effective corporate lobbyists? Personal income tax rates are likewise progressive, but climb steadily upward, from 15 percent to 39.1 percent.

What constitutes taxable income for the corporation? The tax code defines taxable corporate income as the entity's total income

TABLE 4-2

U.S. Federal Taxes Levied on Corporations, 2001

IF TAXABLE INCOME IS

Over	But Not over	Tax Is	Of the Amount over
$0	$50,000	15%	$0
$50,000	$75,000	$7,500 + 25%	$50,000
$75,000	$100,000	$13,750 + 34%	$75,000
$100,000	$335,000	$22,250 + 39%	$100,000
$335,000	$10,000,000	$113,900 + 34%	$335,000
$10,000,000	$15,000,000	$3,400,000 + 35%	$10,000,000
$15,000,000	$18,333,333	$5,150,000 + 38%	$15,000,000
$18,333,333		35%	$0

for the tax period. Total income generally means gross sales receipts, interest income, dividend income, rents received, and royalties *less* all legal deductions. Deductions include the compensation paid to employees, repairs and maintenance to corporate-owned property, rent paid, interest payments to creditors, depreciation, and advertising outlays. The corporation can also deduct its contributions to employee pension and profit-sharing plans, and what it spends on employee benefits. Dividend payments to shareholders are *not* deductible from taxable income.

Within certain limits, U.S. corporations can also deduct foreign income tax paid or accrued, or apply it as a credit against U.S. taxes due. The treatment of profits generated overseas is a major issue for U.S. corporations. The corporations often attempt to keep those profits overseas and not repatriate them for the benefit of the U.S. tax authority. This, however, keeps the immediate benefits of off-shore profits out of the hands of U.S. shareholders.

Marginal Tax Rate

Progressive tax rates underpin the concept of *marginal tax rate,* which you can use to determine the tax benefit of a deductible expense or the tax penalty on the next dollar of taxable income. The marginal tax rate is the rate of tax paid on the next or the last dollar of income. These are the dollars affected by the decisions you make today. Thus, if your corporation has $40,000 in taxable income, its marginal rate is 15 percent. If its taxable income is $20 million, its marginal rate is 35 percent. Once you know your marginal rate, you can determine the after-tax costs of various deductible business expenses and charitable contributions. Here's the formula:

After-Tax Cost = Cost × (1 − Marginal Tax Rate)

To illustrate, consider what a $1,000 corporate contribution to the Angus McDuff Foundation, a tax-deductible organization, is really costing, assuming that the company is in the 35 percent bracket.

$$\text{After-Tax Cost} = \$1{,}000 \times (1 - 0.35)$$
$$= \$1{,}000 \times 0.65$$
$$= \$650$$

Thus, the corporation is only giving up $650 when it makes this contribution, since $350 is saved on its tax obligation. In effect, the tax authority is subsidizing 35 percent of the contribution.

The same method can be used in determining the after-tax benefit of an action or a decision. For instance, if you increased revenues by $1,000 this year by charging more for coffee in the corporate lunchroom, you could calculate the after-tax benefit of that move as $650.

Credits versus Deductions

Periodically, Congress offers tax credits for certain actions and situations. These are designed to motivate certain behaviors, such as job creation in low-income neighborhoods or greater capital investment. Tax credits can be found in both business and individual tax environments.

Some people think of tax credits and tax deductions as the same thing. They are not. Deductions, such as a charitable deduction or an interest expense deduction, allow a corporation or an individual to reduce the level of taxable income. Those deductions become more valuable as the marginal bracket increases. A $1,000 deduction will reduce taxes by $150 for a corporation in the 15 percent bracket; the same deduction produces a $390 tax savings to an entity in the highest bracket. To an individual who makes so little that he or she pays no taxes, a deduction is worth nothing.

A *tax credit,* in contrast, provides a dollar-for-dollar tax saving. Thus, a $1,000 tax credit reduces the tax liability by $1,000—no matter what the tax bracket may be. This is why the U.S. government's use of tax credits to spur investment or the hiring of unskilled people is so appealing to business owners and executives. Up to the limits of these programs, the government is footing the entire bill.

Tax Loss Carryback and Carryforward

Every year that your company produces taxable income, it has to send part of that income off to Washington in the form of corporate income taxes. But what about the years in which losses are incurred? Is there a way to average out years of income and losses for tax purposes?

Fortunately, the U.S. tax code's provision for tax loss carryback and carryforward makes it possible for a company to use losses produced in bad years to recoup some or all of the taxes it paid in the previous good years. It can even carry forward any unused losses into future years, using them to offset tax liabilities incurred then.

Specifically, the law allows an operating loss to be carried back two years, and any still-unused portions to be carried forward twenty years beyond the loss year. (Note: This is the general rule; consult a tax professional about the exceptions.) If an entity chooses to carry back the loss, however, it must first carry the entire loss to the earliest carryback year. If the loss is not used up in that year, the remaining loss must be carried to the next earliest carryback year, and so on. Losses not used during the two carryback years are carried forward in ascending order. There they offset any incurred taxes.

Summing Up

Though this treatment of corporate taxes is by necessity simplified, the information may nevertheless help you make sound business decisions. For example, if you are a sole proprietor or a member of a partnership, it is important to understand the tax implications of changing to a C corporation or an S corporation. Here, the important points to remember are these:

- The taxable income of sole proprietors and partnerships flows directly onto the tax obligations of their owners. There is no "business level" of income taxation. S corporations do the same.

- C corporations and their shareholders are subject to double taxation: The entity is taxed on its earnings, and its shareholders are taxed on any distribution made to them.

The chapter also dealt with the concepts of progressive and marginal rates. Understanding these points is critical for decision makers in all types of for-profit organizations.

As you deal with tax issues, however, always observe these caveats:

- The rules of the game change regularly. Substantive changes to the tax code occur every few years. In addition, tax court and IRS rulings appear sporadically, changing the current understanding about the rules and how they are applied in practice. For this reason, you must keep current with the latest changes.

- Always seek professional advice when taxes are an important element of your decisions.

Financing Operations and Growth

Funding the Different Stages of Growth

Key Topics Covered in This Chapter

- *Start-up financing*

- *Financing current operations*

- *Financing growth*

- *Proper match of assets and financing*

- *Typical financing arrangements*

THIS CHAPTER PROVIDES a broad overview of how businesses use internal and external sources to finance their operations and growth. Several sections use the financing arrangements of eBay, the online auction company, to illustrate how one company has tapped different sources of capital to fuel rapid expansion.

Start-Up Financing

When Angus McDuff started a woodworking business in 1963, he was well prepared for self-employment. His transition from supervisor at a small wooden-lamp-making concern to proprietor of his own business was very direct. As a supervisor, he knew all about shaping and fitting lumber into consumer and commercial products. He knew the materials suppliers on a first-name basis, and he was often in contact with wholesale and retail distributors of his company's finished products.

McDuff had used the last year of his employment productively. In his spare time, he designed a small line of wooden hat racks, used his experience in the lamp business to calculate his production costs, and learned a great deal about the channels of distribution through which his new products would be sold. So, when he walked away from his job and became a business owner, he was extremely well prepared.

Starting the venture, however, required more than knowledge. Financial and production assets were also required. McDuff calculated that he would need enough cash, say, $3,000, to tide him over a three-month start-up period in which the generation of sale revenues was bound to be minimal. He'd also need an inventory of lumber, hardware fixtures, and other materials. Those items of material inventory would be transformed into finished-goods inventory over time. And he'd also need money to pay for an annual property and liability insurance policy and the first three months of rent on a small workshop. As discussed in chapter 1, these items would be McDuff's current assets, whose monetary value is as follows:

Cash		$3,000
Inventory		
Lumber	$800	
Hardware	$700	
Other	$500	
Total inventory		$2,000
Prepaid expenses		
Insurance (1 year)	$800	
Rent (3 months)	$1,500	
Total prepaid expenses		$2,300
Total current assets		$7,300

McDuff's business, which he decided to call Amalgamated Hat Rack Company, needed some fixed assets as well: a wood lathe, a few power and hand tools, workbenches for the shop, and a panel truck for picking up materials and making deliveries to customers. Fortunately, Angus already owned an old panel truck and many of the required tools, and his former employer was glad to sell him two old wood lathes and several surplus workbenches.

With these, Angus was able to complete the fixed-asset section of his balance sheet:

Panel truck	$1,200	
Lathes	$1,200	
Other tools	$300	
Shop fixtures	$300	
Total fixed assets		3,000
Total current assets (from above)		$7,300
Total current and fixed assets		$10,300

Note that the panel truck and other tools are items owned by McDuff. Their value was calculated at these items' market value at the time he placed them in service.

McDuff's requirement of $10,300 in assets might not seem like much, but remember that this was 1963, when a dollar was actually worth something! Fortunately, Angus and his wife, Alice, had some money available in their savings account, they already own the truck and tools, and Alice's uncle offered to contribute the rest as a zero-interest loan of $5,000. "You can pay me back at a thousand per year," he told them. "And good luck with the business." All together, they had the financing they needed to get the business rolling.

And that's how Amalgamated was initially financed. You've already seen the asset side of the balance sheet. Here's how the other side looked in late 1963:

Current liabilities (current portion of five-year loan)	$1,000
Long-term liabilities (five-year loan from Alice's uncle)	$4,000
Total liabilities	$5,000
Owners' equity	$5,300
Total liabilities and owners' equity	$10,300

As you can see, all contributions of capital are represented on the liabilities side of the balance sheet, and the total exactly balances the various assets on the other side.

Many, if not most, small businesses are initially financed in a manner similar to the Amalgamated case—with the owner/operator's personal savings and with contributions from friends and family members. Some individuals even resort to using their credit-card lines of credit for start-up capital, expensive as that is.

Trade Credit

Many small business people obtain thirty- to sixty-day trade credit from their suppliers as one component of their start-up (and ongoing) financing. For instance, a shoe-store owner may be able to obtain $3,000 worth of shoes from a wholesaler, with payment due in sixty days. If she knows her customers and has picked her

inventory wisely, she may be able to sell all or most of the shoes during that sixty-day period and use the proceeds to pay the bill when
it comes due. In effect, the supplier will have financed that portion
of the store's inventory without charge—which is a better deal for
the owner than using a bank line of credit or another device that
involves interest charges. Trade credit, of course, is a current liability
and must be reflected on the balance sheet as follows:

Current assets		Current liabilities	
Inventory	$3,000	Accounts payable	$3,000

If the shoe merchant sells all the shoes for $5,000, then the inventory
drops to zero, but cash increases by $5,000. The accounts payable
amount remains until the bill is paid. There are also income taxes
payable from the sale—in this case figured at $800. And to keep both
sides of the ledger in balance, owners' equity increases by $1,200, as
follows:

Current assets		Current liabilities	
Cash	$5,000	Accounts payable	$3,000
Inventory	$0	Income tax payable	$800
		Owners' equity	$1,200

This is how balance sheets stay balanced as transactions are made.

Commercial Banks

Bankers are justifiably nervous about making loans to start-up businesses, since the failure rate is high. Most local bankers will only
extend loans to a start-up if they are comfortable with the situation
and the qualifications of the borrower.

What makes bank lenders comfortable? Bankers ask Three Big
Questions before they lend money, and rarely part with their capital
if they cannot obtain satisfactory answers to all three:

1. Will the borrower be able to pay me back?

2. Is the borrower's character such that he or she will pay me
   back?

3. If the borrower fails to repay me, are there marketable assets that I can put my hands on?

In seeking an answer to the first of the questions, a banker will evaluate the entrepreneur and the business plan:

- Does the applicant understand the market and have a feasible plan for satisfying it?

- Does the entrepreneur have the experience or knowledge—or both—required to operate this type of business successfully?

- Is the business plan realistic, complete, and based on reasonable assumptions?

- Are the revenue and cost projections realistic and conservative?

The banker will also address the adequacy of the venture's financing, since inadequate financing is a major reason for business failure.

Lenders generally answer the second question, "Is the borrower's character such that he or she will pay me back?" by examining the loan applicant's credit history. Whether it's a car loan, a home mortgage, or a business loan, a banker will seek evidence that the applicant pays his or her bills on schedule.

The third question, "What can I put my hands on?" is about *collateral*. Collateral is an asset pledged to the lender until such time as the loan is satisfied. In an automobile loan, the lender retains title to the vehicle and makes sure that you've made a sufficiently large down payment so that the bank can repossess the car, sell it, and fully reimburse itself from the proceeds if you fail to make timely loan payments. Business loans are similar. The lender wants to see assets that, in the case of business failure, can be sold off to satisfy the loan. Those assets might be current assets such as cash, inventory, and accounts receivable; they might also be fixed assets such as vehicles, buildings, and equipment.

Financing Growth

A startling number of small businesses fail or are bought out by new owners. Of those that remain, most stay small. The corner liquor store, the local auto dealer, the money management firm across the street from your office—even if they survive and prosper, most of these enterprises will not grow substantially larger. If profits grow, most of that growth will be channeled into the bank accounts of the individual owners. These people are not aiming to build empires; they're simply trying to create and sustain good livelihoods.

But every so often, the owner attempts to build on his or her initial success. A liquor-store owner opens a store in an adjacent community. A successful auto dealer takes on a franchise for another line of vehicles and opens a showroom on the other side of town. The successful money management firm hires additional professionals in financial and estate planning to expand its services and cast its net to a wider population of clients.

Some cases of business growth are legendary in their proportions. The late Dave Thomas, creator of Wendy's, followed the example set by Harlan Sanders (Kentucky Fried Chicken) and Ray Kroc (McDonald's), and expanded his fast-food restaurant chain throughout North America. Michael Dell expanded his made-to-order computer business from a one-room operation to the top of the PC heap, outpacing industry giants such as Hewlett-Packard, IBM, and Compaq. eBay, the online auction enterprise, quickly outgrew its founder's apartment, and within the space of seven years was handling billions of dollars' worth of transactions. In each of these cases, financing greased the wheels of growth. And this financing obviously didn't come from the savings accounts of the entrepreneurs, their friends, or their families.

Financing Growth at eBay

Consider eBay, perhaps the most successful company of the dot-com explosion. It grew from a home-based hobby-business to a sizable corporation in a very short time. The company's brief history underscores the role played by different forms of financing.

eBay was started in 1995 by Pierre Omidyar, a young man with experience in software development and online commerce. Omidyar set up his business on a free Web site provided by his Internet service. His only business assets at the time were a filing cabinet, an old school desk, and a laptop computer. His hobby–business grew quickly, which forced him to buy his own server, hire someone to handle billings and the checks that came in the mail, and eventually move the operation from his apartment to a small office. Omidyar and his business partner, Jeff Skoll, soon began paying themselves annual salaries of $25,000.[1]

This early period of growth was essentially self-financed: The cash coming in the mail from transaction fees was sufficient to cover the business's expenses and investments. But a period of explosive growth was right around the corner. By the end of December 2000, this little online company grew from serving a handful of auction devotees to 22 million registered users. By then it offered more than eight thousand product categories; on any given day, the company listed more than 6 million items for sale in an auction–style format and another 8 million items in a fixed–price format. A sizable infra-structure of office space, customer support, proprietary software, information systems, and equipment was required to host a business with this volume and keep it churning. eBay used internally devel-oped systems to operate its auction service and to process transac-tions, including billing and collections. Those systems had to be con-tinually improved and expanded as the pace of transactions on the site increased.

To keep the wheels of growth turning, the company spent liber-ally on new site features and categories. eBay incurred $4.6 million in product development expenses in 1998, $24.8 million in 1999, and $55.9 million in 2000. Even larger sums were spent on market-ing, brand development, and acquisitions aimed at broadening the company's services and extending its reach to other parts of the world.

Before long, eBay had expanded its balance–sheet assets dramat-ically. Here are a few highlights (rounded to millions) from the company's 10-K report for the fiscal year ending December 31, 2000:

Cash and cash equivalents: $202 million

Short-term investments: $354 million

Long-term investments: $218 million

Total assets: $1,182 million

With total assets of nearly $1.2 billion, eBay was light-years away from Pierre Omidyar's apartment office.

On the other side of the ledger are the following items from the same 2000 balance sheet:

Current liabilities and long-term debt: $169 million

Total stockholders' equity: $1,014 million

Current and long-term liabilities in this case are amazingly small relative to the magnitude of eBay's assets. So, recalling the balance-sheet equation

Assets = Liabilities + Stockholders' Equity

you can see that a large percentage of those assets are claimed by shareholders—in fact, 86 percent.

By digging a bit deeper, we find that eBay's remarkable growth was principally financed in two ways: first, by cash flows from operations (self-financing) and, second, by external financing. Let's examine these sources individually, since they are so important to growing companies.

eBay's Cash Flows from Operations

As described in chapter 1, a cash flow statement totals the cash flow entering and leaving the enterprise as a result of operations, investments, and financing activities. Table 5-1 shows the highlights from eBay's cash flow statement for the years 1998 through 2000.

The first row, net cash provided by operating activities, shows that the company ran some portion of its operations and paid people's salaries, taxes, and other bills (operating activities) from operating cash flow. What's more, the level of positive cash flow from operations grew substantially from year to year, helping to fund

TABLE 5-1

eBay's Cash Flow, 1998 through 2000 (in Thousands of Dollars)

	2000	1999	1998
Net Cash Provided by Operating Activities	100,148	62,852	6,041
Net Cash Used in Investing Activities	(206,054)	(603,363)	(53,024)
Net Cash Provided by Financing Activities	85,978	725,027	72,159
Net Increase (Decrease) in Cash and Cash Equivalents	(19,928)	184,516	25,176
Cash and Cash Equivalents at End of Year (After Accounting for Beginning Balance)	201,873	221,801	37,285

Source: eBay 10-K report, 2000.

growth. Thus, an important portion of eBay's asset growth was financed internally, from its successful and profitable operations. Instead of returning even a cent of that cash to shareholders in the form of dividends, it plowed everything back into the business. That is typical of fast-growing firms.

eBay's External Financing

Internally generated cash was sufficient to finance operations in the early days, but not nearly sufficient to fund eBay's meteoric growth. Large as they were, eBay's cash flows from operations paled in comparison to the cash outflows caused by investments during the same period. In the best of those years (2000), cash flow from operations covered slightly less than half of the investment outflow. To make up the difference, the company had to resort to external financing (depicted in the line labeled "Net cash provided by financing activities").

eBay's financial statements (too voluminous to show here) indicate that almost all of its external financing took the form of stockholders' capital—that is, the company and its subsidiaries raised cash by selling shares (almost all common shares) to investors. The first of these was a $5 million private placement with Benchmark Capital, a

Silicon Valley venture capital firm. In return for its cash, Benchmark was given a 22 percent equity interest in eBay. The next big capital-raising event in eBay's history was its 1998 *initial public offering* (IPO). As the name clearly states, an IPO is a corporation's first offering of its shares to the public. An IPO is a major milestone in a corporation's life cycle in that the offering marks the company's transition from a private to a public enterprise. As we'll see in a later chapter, this new status opens up much larger opportunities to raise equity capital. The universe of potential capital contributors expands from the small and clubby circle of private investors to a much broader group of individual investors, mutual funds, and retirement funds. But it isn't a picnic! Being public subjects the company to far greater regulation and scrutiny. Suddenly (in the United States), the company must file regular, periodic reports with the Securities and Exchange Commission, and the CEO and CFO must spend substantial time making presentations to institutional investors and securities analysts.

An IPO is also an opportunity for the existing investors, including the venture capitalists and shareholding employees, to cash in some or all of their shares—turning paper certificates into real money. eBay's Omidyar, for example, held over 44 million shares of his company's common stock before its IPO. In the wake of the IPO and the stock price run-up in the months that followed, Omidyar became a billionaire four times over. The value of Benchmark's shares rose to the point that it could claim a 49,000 percent return on its investment—one for the record books!

eBay's financial managers and investment bankers used the company's high stock price and public appetite for shares to float another common stock issue in 1999. This one netted the company more than $700 million, most of which was used in the company's campaign of expansion.

Other Forms of External Financing

Thus far in this chapter, we've described supplier trade credit, bank loans, and common stock issues as important forms of external

financing. Today's corporations also use a few other important forms
of financing:

Commercial paper. Large corporations with high credit ratings often use the sale of commercial paper to finance their
short-term requirements. They use it as a lower-cost alternative to short-term bank borrowing. *Commercial paper* is a
short-term debt security, generally reaching maturity in 2 to
270 days. Most paper is sold at a discount to its face value and
is redeemable at face value on maturity. The difference
between the discounted sale price and the face value represents interest to the purchaser of the paper. Investors with
temporary cash surpluses are the usual purchasers of commercial paper; for them it is a reasonably safe way to obtain a
return on their idle cash.

Bonds. A bond is also a debt security (IOU), usually issued
with a fixed interest rate and a stated maturity date. The bond
issuer has a contractual obligation to make periodic interest
payments and to redeem the bond at its face value on maturity. Bonds may have short-, intermediate-, or long-term
maturities (e.g., from one to thirty years). Generally, they pay
a fixed interest rate on a semiannual basis. Chapter 6 covers
bonds in greater detail.

Preferred stock. This type of equity security is similar to a
bond in that it pays a stated dividend to the shareholder each
year, and once the shares begin trading in the secondary
market, then the share prices, like bonds, fluctuate with
changes in market interest rates and the creditworthiness of
the issuer. Also like bonds, preferred stock is used by some
corporations as an external form of equity financing. Preferred stock will be discussed in greater detail in chapter 6.

The Matching of Assets and Financing

One of the principles of financing—whether to start a company,
maintain its operations, or advance its growth—is to make a proper

match between the assets and their associated forms of financing. The general principle is to finance current (i.e., short-term) assets with short-term financing, and long-term assets with long-term or permanent financing.

The use of supplier trade credit for financing inventory, as described earlier in this chapter, is an example of matching short-term assets with short-term financing. The shoe-store owner matched sixty-day financing against an asset that she believed would be sold within that period. Likewise, eBay financed its sizable infrastructure of office space, customer support, proprietary software, systems, and equipment with capital supplied by shareholders—a permanent form of financing. We could identify countless other enterprises that follow this sensible principle. When states and municipalities build bridges, hockey stadiums, water treatment plants, and so forth, they typically finance them with twenty- to thirty-year bonds—financing vehicles whose maturities roughly match the productive life of the assets.

To understand why this principle is so important, consider first what might happen if you tried to finance the purchase of your new home (a long-term asset) with an 8 percent, non-amortizing $200,000 loan that came due in just three years. Under the terms of the loan, you'd pay $16,000 in annual interest, and then be obligated to repay the $200,000 at the end of the third year. This would be feasible *if* you could negotiate another loan at the end of three years to replace the one that's due, and *if* interest rates were still affordable. But that's two *if*s. Money might become so tight that you could not locate a new lender when you needed one, or the lender you did find might want 10 or 12 percent. In either case, foreclosure would be likely. You couldn't operate with such a situation, and neither can a business enterprise.

The opposite mismatch situation—borrowing long to finance a short-term asset—is just as bad. Some people take out second mortgages on their homes to finance a dream vacation. Such are the temptations of home equity loans. The vacation will soon be over, but the payments will go on and on. In business, we expect that the assets we acquire with borrowed money will produce incremental

revenues (or cost savings) at rates and over periods more than sufficient to pay off their financing costs. The same can be said for
owners' capital.

A Life–Cycle View of Financing

Is your company still in the start-up phase? Is it a mature enterprise
that has already exploited most of its growth potential? Or is it
somewhere between these two extremes? It is useful to stand back
and observe the theoretical life cycle of business inception, growth,
and maturity. Doing so helps us understand how and when different
forms of financing—and different financing institutions—come into
play. We've already observed some of this in our descriptions of
Amalgamated Hat Rack, a fictional entity, and eBay, currently the
strongest of the new Internet-based businesses. Here, we consider a
more general case, divided arbitrarily into four phases: Start-up,
Growth 1, Growth 2, and Maturity (figure 5-1).

Start–Up

Amalgamated Hat Rack is a fairly typical entrepreneurial business
start-up. The founder/manager in this phase must scratch around for
the capital needed to acquire assets and to finance operations. This
capital generally comes from personal savings, loans or equity from
friends and relatives, and, in some instances, from local "angels"—
businesspeople who recognize an opportunity and want to participate as either lenders or minority owners. A local bank may also
extend some funds if there is adequate collateral. Although many
companies in this phase are incorporated, their shares are usually
held by only a handful of individuals, and those shares have no real
market.

Growth 1

During this phase, the business expands it sales and develops a base of
reliable customers. As a result, more capital is typically required.

FIGURE 5-1

A Life-Cycle View of Financing

Revenues

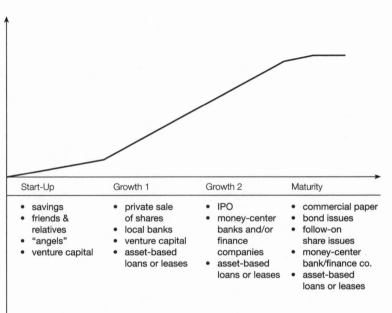

Start-Up	Growth 1	Growth 2	Maturity

• savings
• friends &
  relatives
• "angels"
• venture capital
	• private sale
	  of shares
	• local banks
	• venture capital
	• asset-based
	  loans or leases
		• IPO
		• money-center
		  banks and/or
		  finance
		  companies
		• asset-based
		  loans or leases
			• commercial paper
			• bond issues
			• follow-on
			  share issues
			• money-center
			  bank/finance co.
			• asset-based
			  loans or leases

Some capital, as we've seen in eBay's case, is generated through reinvested profits from operations. But more is needed if growth is strong. By having proven its credibility as a business operation, the enterprise can generally tap external capital more easily than it could previously.

Debt capital in this phase often comes from local banks, whereas equity capital is gathered through the private sale of shares to local investors. The business is still too small to become a public company. As a result, it cannot tap broader equity markets. If the company is in a "hot" growth industry, or if it is close to producing a breakthrough with some proprietary, game-changing product, it many gain the attention of a venture capitalist.

About Venture Capitalists

A venture capitalist (VC) or a VC firm is a high-risk investor who seeks an equity position in a start-up or an early-growth company with high potential. In return for capital, the VC typically takes a significant percentage of ownership of the business and a position on its board. VCs are much engaged in the strategic management of their fledgling companies and are often instrumental in connecting them with suppliers and potential business allies. In many cases, they recruit the technical and managerial personnel these companies need to succeed.

VCs are not content with the 15 to 20 percent annual returns that would thrill most common stock investors. Knowing that they are bound to strike out on many of their deals, they seek a huge return on every venture. Generally, VCs seek out small firms with the potential to return ten times their risk capital within five years. Most aim to "harvest" their investments during the initial public offering or follow-on issues of company share, and move on to the next opportunity.

In the lore of American venture capitalism, "General" Georges Doriot, a Harvard Business School professor, is fondly remembered. Doriot organized the first venture capital fund, American Research & Development (ARD), in the late 1940s to benefit from the many small, high-tech companies being incubated in the research laboratories of Harvard and MIT. His biggest score was with Digital Equipment Corporation (DEC), a company founded by Kenneth Olsen, a young MIT-trained engineer. Sensing an opportunity, Doriot invested $70,000 in DEC in 1957. By 1971, when Doriot cashed in, that investment had grown to $355 million.

Growth 2

Most companies never get beyond the first phase of growth. But those that do have access to a broader spectrum of financing opportunities—in particular, public stock and bond markets. In a sense this second phase of growth is experienced by companies that have proven their revenue-generating abilities to traditional financing sources. The prospect of further growth is a powerful lure to equity investors, who hope to buy shares while the shares are still cheap and unrecognized—and hang on for a profitable ride.

Local banks are also important sources of external financing at this stage. The business now has a confidence-inspiring record of producing revenues and paying its bills. And it has assets that it can pledge as collateral. The company may also have grown so much that it has outgrown the lending capacity of its local bank, in which case it can move upstream to a large money-center bank.

The major moment in the Growth 2 phase is the IPO, which we described in the preceding eBay example. IPOs are managed by one or more investment banking firms selected by the issuing company. The investment bankers help the issuing company through the strict regulatory requirements of issuing shares to the public. More important, the investment bank and its syndicate of broker-dealers (stockbrokers) provide direct access to millions of potential investors: individual investors, mutual funds, pension funds, and private money managers. Chapter 6 has more information on investment bankers.

Distributing shares through an IPO is expensive, involving substantial fees paid to accountants and lawyers, and a big cut to the investment bank and its syndicate. But a successful IPO is the financial equivalent of a blood transfusion. Suddenly, the company's coffers are flush with cash that it can use to pay off loans, buy back preferred stocks it might have issued and now regrets, and finance its next round of growth.

Maturity

Trees do not grow to the skies. Nor do growth companies continue growing forever. Eventually, growth tapers off for one or more reasons:

- Success and profitability draw competitors into the market

- Demand for the product or service is largely satisfied (market saturation)

- A technological shift

- A loss of ambition, agility, or innovation as the organization grows larger and older

Whatever the cause, few companies sustain high growth rates for more than a decade. This does not mean that growth necessarily stops and that continued financing is not needed. Even saturated markets for mature products such as automobiles continue to expand incrementally as the population increases and as people in undeveloped countries become more affluent and demand them. And for a $1 billion enterprise, even a 3 percent growth in revenues may require additional financing. Then, too, mature companies are often involved in mergers, acquisitions, restructuring, or other activities, all of which have important financing implications.

Assuming that the mature company is creditworthy, it has many options for additional external financing. For short-term needs, it can issue commercial paper, tap its bank lines of credit, or negotiate a term loan with a bank or other financial institutions, such as insurance companies and pension funds. The mature company can use its existing assets and cash flow as collateral to lower the cost of loans. Alternatively, the company can obtain significant funds through the sale-and-leaseback arrangements described in chapter 3.

The healthy, mature company also enjoys access to public capital markets for debt (bonds) and equity capital (shares). Here, timing is all-important. The company naturally wants to sell its bonds when interest rates are low and sell its shares when its share price is high.

Summing Up

This chapter has described how operations and growth are typically financed at different phases in the life cycle of business enterprises. In the start-up phase, they generally depend on the following sources for financing:

- Personal savings and lines of credit

- Loans from friends and relatives

- Thirty- to sixty-day trade credit from suppliers

- Loans from commercial banks

- Venture capitalists (usually reserved for high-profile start-ups)

Companies that are experiencing growth face the challenge of finding the financing to support it. Growing companies generally rely on some combination of internally generated funds and external financing from the sale of equity (shares) or the sale of debt (commercial paper, bonds, or preferred stock). We have not discussed the roles played by the money and capital markets, which are the subject of chapter 6.

6

Money and Capital Markets

Another Option for Funding Growth

Key Topics Covered in This Chapter

- *Money markets*

- *Capital markets—both primary and secondary*

- *Common and preferred stocks*

- *Bonds*

C HAPTER 5 DESCRIBED how business assets are financed through a combination of internally generated cash flow, short-term liabilities and debt, long-term debt, retained earnings, and the capital of owners. This chapter is concerned with the markets through which nonbank debt financing and equity capital are obtained, specifically the money and capital markets. In the course of this discussion, you'll learn how securities are issued in collaboration with investment bankers. You'll also learn the basics of the capital market securities typically used by corporations to raise funds: stock and various forms of debt.

Money and capital markets (collectively, financial markets) were once local or national in scope; today they span the globe, linking users and suppliers of capital with the speed of electronic trading. Those links channel capital to what appear to be its highest uses. Thus, a Chicago-area manufacturer with plans for a new factory but insufficient funds may be linked through the capital markets with a German investor who wants to obtain a higher return on idle capital. Likewise, a mutual-fund portfolio manager in Boston can channel some of her cash through the same capital market to a promising enterprise in Taiwan.

Access to money and capital markets is to contemporary economies what access to food and water is to a living organism—a source of vitality, regeneration, and growth. This role was demonstrated in the decline and eventual collapse of the economy of the Soviet bloc in the waning years of the twentieth century. Western economies and their trading partners in the Far East benefited immensely from open and efficient financial markets. Thanks to those markets, cash and long-term capital were shifted away from stagnating enterprises and industries toward others with better technologies, superior management, and brighter futures. The Soviet bloc, meanwhile, had no such mechanism for moving its own cash and capital and stood outside the network of Western finance. In its stead, Soviet-bloc economies depended on cronyism and the dubious judgment of politicians and state bureaucrats to allocate capital. The result was the use of scarce capital to prop up failing industries—and eventual collapse.

Money Markets

When corporations need short-term financing to get through seasonal business cycles or for other purposes, they often turn to the *money market*. Marcia Stigum and Frank Fabozzi have a good definition of the money market: "a market in which large borrowers raise short-term money by selling various debt instruments; that is, it is a 'new issues' market for short-term securities. The money market is also a secondary market in which such securities, once issued, are actively traded."[1]

Money markets, then, are the institutions and trading channels through which short-term debt instruments are originated and distributed. In the United States, those instruments include:

- **Certificates of deposit:** time deposits with a specified maturity and interest rate, issued by banks and marketable through a secondary market of brokers

- **Commercial paper:** unsecured IOUs sold at discounts to face value

- **U.S. Treasury bills (T-bills):** negotiable debt securities with maturities of one year or less; sold at discounts to face value

- **Discounted notes:** notes issued by the Federal Home Loan Bank and other government agencies

These financial instruments have two things in common: They are highly liquid (i.e., they can be easily sold to other investors for cash), and they represent very low risk credit to investors. A corporation like Amalgamated Hat Rack, which has more cash than it needs for a month or more, can safely invest in these instruments with the expectation that it will get its money back *plus* receive a decent amount of interest. If Amalgamated determines that it cannot hold these instruments until their maturity, then the company's treasurer can sell them in the secondary market. On the other side of the same transaction, some other entity (the U.S. Treasury, another government agency, or a public corporation) is using the money market to sell its short-term IOUs with the goal of obtaining capital.

Where is the money market located? In truth, the money market is nowhere in particular. It is a worldwide network of dealers—mostly money-center banks located in major Western financial centers—that buy and sell for their own accounts. The global span of the market has the effect of establishing fairly uniform worldwide rates for short-term debt. Thus, a corporation that wants to sell its commercial paper for the lowest possible interest rate can sometimes bypass high local rates and sell its paper where rates for the same maturity and risk factors are lower. The place may be on the other side of the country or the other side of the globe. Any corporation or individual can invest in money-market instruments. But the reverse is not the case. Only the largest, most creditworthy corporations can sell their paper through the money market. Entities such as Amalgamated are too small to be issuers.

Capital Markets

The term *capital markets* describes the markets in which long-term debt instruments (bonds) and equity securities (shares of stock)—including private placements—are issued and traded. Like the money market, capital markets include primary and secondary components. The primary market consists of securities dealers and financial institutions that issue newly minted securities to the investing public. The secondary market includes both these primary market dealers plus a network of over-the-counter dealers (e.g., NASDAQ) and organized securities exchanges such as the New York Stock Exchange and Tokyo Stock Exchange. The secondary market provides opportunities for the buying and selling of securities after their initial issuance.

The Primary Market: eBay Revisited

To understand how capital markets work, let's return to our earlier discussion of eBay, the online auction company, which first began operations in the apartment of its founder in 1995. The company was incorporated as eBay Inc. in California in May 1996. Up to this point, its growth was essentially self-financed through internal cash flows. A year later, it sold a 22 percent ownership stake to the venture capital firm Benchmark Capital in return for $5 million.

Thus far, eBay's financing had been entirely private—and outside the realm of the main capital markets. Even a subsequent sale of a series of preferred shares was privately placed to a set of well-heeled private investors.

As described in chapter 5, eBay first tapped the public capital markets for financing in September 1998 with the initial public offering of common stock. How this IPO was accomplished is both typical and instructive in the ways of the primary market for corporate shares. Like other corporations eager to tap the deep pools of equity capital, eBay enlisted the aid of an investment banking firm—in this case Goldman Sachs.

An investment bank is not like the more familiar commercial bank. It is not in the business of taking deposits from savers and making loans. Instead, it acts as an agent and a deal maker for very substantial business entities seeking capital. In return for a tidy fee and a piece of the action, the investment bank has several roles:

- **Helping the issuing corporation get its regulatory act together.** Specifically, the investment bank helps the corporation get through the stringent regulatory hurdles that go hand in hand

with issuing securities. These hurdles include the development
of a prospectus—called a red herring. In its preliminary form,
the prospectus must provide full disclosure about the company,
its business, and its finances to potential investors.

- **Pricing the securities being offered.** When shares are being
  offered to the public for the first time, no one knows for certain how they should be priced. Because the shares haven't
  been traded back and forth by willing buyers and sellers, there
  is no certainty as to a market-clearing price. The capital-
  seeking corporation would naturally want its shares priced as
  high as the market will bear—doing so will maximize the cash
  that goes into its coffers. But investors expect a new issue to be
  priced at a per-share amount that represents something of a
  bargain compared to seasoned securities. Having expertise in
  this difficult pricing area, the investment bank must mediate
  between these disparate objectives.

- **Arranging for the distribution of shares.** The issuing corporation may have the shares, but the investment bank has access to
  potential purchasers for them. By putting together a syndicate
  of distributing broker-dealers, the investment bank assures that
  it can "move the merchandise" into the portfolios of pension
  funds, mutual funds, and individual investors. In most cases, the
  investment bank takes the shares off the hands of the issuing
  corporation at a given price, marks them up to some predetermined profitable level, and uses its own distribution channels
  and those of its syndicate partners to sell them to the investing
  public. In this sense the investment bank underwrites the risk
  of selling millions of shares.

That, in a nutshell, describes the role of an investment bank in an
initial public offering. In eBay's case, Goldman Sachs was the lead
underwriter of a group of investment banks that included Bancamer-
ica Robinson Stephens and BT Alex Brown—all major players.

In the period leading up to eBay's IPO, its CEO and CFO conducted a ten-day, twenty-one-city road show, a series of presenta-

tions to the investment community. A road show is standard procedure with equity issues; it is designed to explain the issuing company's business and generate interest in the offering.

The investment climate at that time was decidedly mixed. The Dow Jones Industrial Average was trending downward, and the Nasdaq composite index was meandering beneath the 2,000 mark. The great high-tech/dot-com boom that would send the Nasdaq composite into the 5,000 area was still over the horizon. Nevertheless, believing that the time was right, eBay and its investment bankers went forward with the offering on September 24, 1998. According to the company's 10-K, slightly more than 4 million shares were sold, netting the fledgling company more than $66 million. These funds went into the war chest that eBay management would use to finance its growth in the years ahead.

The Secondary Market

Once the shares of publicly owned corporations are issued through a primary distribution, they begin trading in what is called the secondary market. The secondary market comprises stock and bond exchanges such as the New York Stock Exchange and networks of over-the-counter securities dealers that buy and sell for their own accounts. Nasdaq is an example of such a network.

In terms of corporate finance, the issuing company receives no proceeds from transactions that take place in the secondary market. Even though there may be plenty of furious buying and selling, and even though a company's share price may skyrocket once it begins trading, none of its changing value accrues to the company. It is all exchanged between buying and selling shareholders.

This is not to say that corporations are indifferent to their share prices in the secondary trading markets. Corporate management is in fact eager to see that its share prices are high and rising. On one level, their interest is personal. Most executives and board members and many rank-and-file employees are owners of their companies' shares or hold options to purchase them; their personal fortunes rise and fall with trading prices.

At the corporate policy level, there are also substantial financing opportunities bound up with a healthy stock price. First, many corporations finance their growth-oriented acquisitions with some combination of cash and a block of their shares. For example, a corporation may purchase another company with $100 million in cash and a half-million shares of its own common shares. Thus, the higher the share price, the greater the purchasing company's buying power. Second, growing companies periodically find it necessary to return to the market for more equity capital. That is, they raise additional capital by issuing more shares to the public. eBay's recent history provides examples of both motivations.

eBay's IPO was priced at what now appears a bargain-basement price—roughly $8 (as adjusted for subsequent splits). Once those shares began trading over-the-counter, enthusiastic bidding pushed that price up dramatically. The dot-com frenzy that followed, and eBay's unique position as the only major online venture actually making a profit, did the rest. Within six months, the company's share price had multiplied roughly fifteenfold.

Fast-expanding eBay employed its high share price as a form of currency and used it to fund a spate of acquisitions. In May 1999, for example, it made three significant acquisitions, each aimed at increasing the breadth of its core business. These were Butterfield & Butterfield, an established live auction house, which eBay acquired for approximately 1.3 million shares of eBay common stock. Kruse, Inc., a specialist in classic car auctions, was another. It too was acquired entirely with eBay common stock. So too was Billpoint, a small company that had developed a billing and payment solution that permitted individuals and small merchants to accept credit cards as payment for Internet-based sales transactions. Not a penny of cash was used in these deals.

Eager to continue with its expansion, in 1999 eBay's management capitalized again on its high share price—this time in another offering of 5 million new shares. The 1999 event added more than $713 million in additional equity capital to the balance sheet. Thus, although none of the trading proceeds of secondary-market activity accrue to their listed companies, a strong stock price facilitates other forms of financing, as the eBay example illustrates.

Capital Market Securities

Now that you understand how the capital markets work, let's consider the basic types of securities that corporations issue to the investing public to raise capital for operations and expansion. Three that you should know are *common stock, preferred stock,* and *bonds.*

Common Stock

Common stock is the class you generally think of whenever stocks are discussed. Each share of common stock represents a fractional ownership interest in the corporation that issued it. Here are the notable features of common stock:

- **Voting rights.** Owners typically are entitled to vote on the selection of board members and on other matters. Some classes of common stock, however, have either no voting rights or limited voting rights.

- **Dividends.** A share of stock entitles its holders to receive dividends on a pro rata basis. Thus, if you owned 5 percent of the outstanding shares of a corporation, you'd be entitled to receive 5 percent of all dividends declared by its board of directors.

- **Residual ownership.** Common shareholders stand at the very end of the line in terms of distributions in cases of liquidation. Their interests are subordinate to the creditors and bondholders to whom the corporation is contractually bound to repay. The claims of unsecured and secured creditors, bondholders, and preferred shareholders must be settled first.

Preferred Stock

Preferred stock is a form of stock that, not unlike a bond, pays a specified dividend. Further, preferred shareholders stand in line ahead of common shareholders with respect to any payment of dividends and any distribution of assets in liquidation. This means, among other things, that the corporation cannot distribute a penny of dividends to common shareholders until it has satisfied its dividend obligation

About Dividends

A *dividend* is a distribution of after-tax corporate earnings to shareholders. Dividends are declared by the corporation's board of directors. The board is under no contractual obligation to common shareholders to declare a dividend. Typically, it will choose to retain all or most after-tax earnings in the business if those funds are needed for profitable growth. Financial theorists maintain that corporate earnings should be distributed when and if the corporation's investment returns are less promising than those that individual shareholders could obtain on their own. This idea is complicated by the requirement that shareholders pay a second tax on earnings distributed as dividends.

Dividends are generally paid in cash and on a quarterly basis, but may also take the form of additional shares. Thus, an owner of one thousand shares may receive an additional ten shares in lieu of a cash dividend. In one case, a prominent whisky producer issued its dividend in kind, sending bottles of its product to shareholders!

to preferred shareholders.

Despite their superior position relative to common shares, preferred stocks have several drawbacks. They generally carry limited or no voting rights. And with the exception of convertible preferreds and rare "participating preferred" shares, preferred shareholders do not benefit from the expanding fortunes of the business. Also, unlike common shares, most preferred shares are callable by the issuer—that is, the issuing corporation may redeem them at a particular price if it is to its advantage.

Preferred stock is unappealing to many capital-seeking U.S. corporate financial managers. The reason has to do with the U.S. tax code, which allows the corporation to deduct the interest it pays on debt but not on the dividends it pays to shareholders. Because of this, dividends (to both preferred and common shareholders) are paid out of after-tax earnings. Faced with this situation, most CFOs would rather raise capital by selling bonds—whose interest they can deduct—than by issuing preferred shares, whose dividend outlays are nondeductible.

Bonds

A *bond* is a capital market debt security. The traditional bond has these features:

- A face value, usually $1,000 or multiples thereof

- A maturity date on which the issuer must repay (i.e., redeem) the bond at its face value; newly issued bonds have maturities from one to thirty years

- An annual fixed interest rate (e.g., 5 percent of the face value), usually payable at six-month intervals, either via coupons or through direct payment to the bondholder

In addition to this traditional form, financial engineering has produced dozens of variations of the bond, each designed to serve the financing needs of particular issuers and to appeal to one or more types of investor. Here are a few notable variations:

- **Zero–coupon bond.** This type of bond has a stated face value and maturity, but has no stated interest rate and makes no periodic payments. Instead, it is issued at a discount to face value, which is paid at maturity. The implied interest is the difference between the issue price and the value at maturity. For example, if a zero–coupon bond is issued for $700 with a face value of $1,000 and 5-year maturity, then the compound annual rate of return to the investor works out to 7.4 percent.

- **Convertible bond.** This type of bond is generally issued with an interest rate that is less than the market rate for "straight" bonds. The issuer can get away with this because this bond contains a provision whereby the holder can convert the bond into a specified number of common shares at a specified price.

Thus, the bondholder receives interest on his or her capital *and* has an opportunity to benefit from the issuer's future good fortunes. Generally, this type of bond is issued with a conversion price that is higher than the company's current stock price.

From a corporate financing perspective, convertibles can be attractive. They bring in long-term capital at less-than-market interest rates (the payment of which is also tax-deductible). And if the company's stock price should rise significantly, then the bondholders will convert to common stock, eliminating the corporation's obligation to make interest payments and to redeem the face value of the bonds. Creditors are converted into shareholders without cost or bother. Typically, the higher stock price is a consequence of corporate growth.

- **Floating– and adjustable–rate notes.** During periods of volatile interest rates, fixed-rate interest bonds are difficult to issue. Even when their stated rates are high, investors worry that rates will go still higher, depressing the market value of these bonds. CFOs are not keen on issuing bonds with high interest rates in any case, since doing so ties them into high, long-term interest expenses. One solution is the floating- or adjustable-rate note, whose interest rate is pegged to a stipulated rate index and adjusted at prescribed intervals. For example, an adjustable-rate note might be issued with an interest rate of 6 percent, with a contractual arrangement that the rate will be readjusted on the first business day of each year to the current average yield on ten-year U.S. Treasury bonds plus ½ percent. Floating-rate notes assure investors that they will receive the current market rate of interest and that their securities will hold their value in the secondary market. What's more, these bonds assure corporate financial managers that they will incur no greater interest expense than what the interest rate climate demands.

Like equity securities, bonds have primary and secondary markets. They are issued into the primary (new-issue) market with the aid of investment banks and their distribution syndicates of broker-dealers. Pricing a bond issue, however, is less challenging than pricing an IPO of shares since bond pricing is largely a function of three factors: (1) the creditworthiness of the issuer, (2) the prevailing market interest rate for bonds with the same credit rating and maturities, and (3) the anticipated liquidity of the bond in the secondary market.

Creditworthiness, or default risk, deserves special attention here. Debt obligations of the U.S. government are considered risk-free as to repayment, since it is believed that the government would never default on its own obligations. Corporate issuers of debt are another matter. They can—and sometimes do—default on their obligations to debt holders. In measuring creditworthiness, investors rely on the ratings assigned to different issues by a handful of commercial rating companies: Moody's, Standard & Poor's, Duff & Phelps, and Fitch Investors Service. Moody's, for example, rates debt securities with the following classification: Aaa, Aa, A, Baa, Ba, B, Caa, Ca, C. Those rated Aaa represent the highest quality, whereas the C rating is attached to debt securities with little probability of any investment value. Naturally, an issuer with a B rating will have to price new-issue bonds at a higher interest rate than will a firm with an A rating, even though the maturity and other terms of the bond are identical. Investors insist on a greater return for a greater amount of risk.

Once a new issue of bonds is issued through a primary distribution, they may begin trading in the secondary market. There, the prices are bound to fluctuate as market interest rates change, the credit ratings of particular issuers change, and as individual bonds move closer to maturity.

Summing Up

This chapter has described the money and capital markets to which corporations turn for funding.

- The money market is the financing source to which they turn when they need short-term debt funding. In the United States,

the debt instruments originated and distributed via the money
market are certificates of deposit, corporate commercial paper,
U.S. T-bills, and the discounted notes of the Federal Home
Loan Bank and other government agencies.

- The capital markets are those in which long-term debt (bonds)
  and equity securities (shares of stock) are issued and traded.

As described in the chapter, the money and capital markets are a
playing field in which four very different sets of participants meet:

1. Business entities—the users of capital—come to the money
   market to obtain short-term financing and competitive rates;
   they come to the capital markets for intermediate and long-
   term capital.

2. Investment bankers act as their coaches and agents in seeking
   these funds.

3. Institutional and individual investors approach these markets
   with their own goals: They seek returns on their capital com-
   mensurate with the known risks.

4. Government regulators—notably the Securities and Exchange
   Commission in the United States—act as referees, doing what
   they can to assure an even playing field characterized by full
   and complete disclosure.

The effective interaction of these four sets of players assures a free
flow of capital to it highest uses.

7

Budgeting

Forecasting Your Company's Financial Future

Key Topics Covered in This Chapter

- *Essential functions of budgeting*

- *Types of budgets and their purposes*

- *Creating an operating budget*

- *Creating a cash budget*

- *Applying sensitivity analysis to budgets*

G OOD GRIEF, IT'S BUDGETING time again" is a common refrain among managers. Budgeting can cause stress and conflict and can eat up lots of hours. But good budgets are worth the time and trouble.

If you are the owner or manager of a small company with few cash resources, a good budget can be the difference between financial success and insolvency—or the business's inability to expand to its full potential. The budgeting process forces you to estimate how many of each product or service you will produce and sell, the cost of those items, the pace at which receivables will be collected, general expenses, and taxes. These figures give that person a forecast of the months or year ahead. A good budget helps you assess whether or not the business will have adequate financial resources to stay the course. For big businesses, forecasting and budgeting provide a similar benefit. And the resulting budget—for individual operation units and for the business as a whole—can be a powerful control mechanism. A budget is also an action plan that guides organizations to their strategic goals.

In this chapter, you'll learn about the many kinds of budgets that serve very different purposes and kinds of businesses. You'll also learn how to determine which type of budget will most effectively help you meet your business goals.

What Is Budgeting?

Before you go on a trip, you fill your bag with the clothes, food, and money you'll need. Budgeting is conceptually similar—planning your trip and ensuring that you'll have sufficient resources to make it to your destination. An organization plans its journey toward its strategic objectives in a similar fashion, and it prepares for the journey with an action plan called a budget. A budget can accomplish various tasks:

- **Cover a short time span.** For example, a start-up company develops a budget to ensure that it will have enough cash to cover operating expenses for the next month or two.

- **Take a long-term perspective.** For example, a pharmaceutical firm builds a multiyear budget for developing a new product.

- **Focus on required resources for a specific project.** For example, if a manufacturing firm needs to install machinery to achieve production efficiencies, then its budget will plot the costs for the project.

- **Account for income as well as expenditures.** For example, a retailer creates a profit plan based on an expected increase in sales.

So what is a *budget*? It is the translation of strategic plans into measurable quantities that express the expected resources required and anticipated returns over a certain period. A budget functions as an action plan. It may also present the estimated future financial statements of the organization. Finally, a budget is an adaptable tool for management to use to achieve its strategic goals.

Budget Functions

Budgets perform four basic functions, each of which is critical to the success of a company in achieving its strategic objectives. These functions are planning, coordinating and communicating, monitoring progress, and evaluating performance.

Planning

Planning is a three-step process to ensure that the organization will have the resources available to achieve its goals:

1. **Choosing goals.** The goals could be as comprehensive as the strategic mission of the organization. For example, as a manager at an Internet service provider (ISP), your goal could be "to be the most efficient provider of Internet services for our valued customers." Or, as the manager of a major-league baseball team, your goal could be specific and very focused: to increase revenues by 10 percent during the next quarter.

2. **Reviewing options and predicting results.** Once the goals have been determined, the next step is to look at the options available for attaining the goals and predict what the most likely outcomes would be for each option. For example, if your goal as a manager at an ISP is to become the most efficient provider of Internet services, then you could opt to maintain state-of-the-art equipment at all times, train the most skilled repair teams in the field, or concentrate on providing the most timely customer service. Or, as a baseball team manager planning to increase revenues by 10 percent, you could consider raising prices, expanding your marketing program, or reducing player acquisition costs. Thus, predicting the costs and benefits of each option is part of planning.

3. **Deciding on options.** After an analysis of the potential costs and benefits of each option, the next step is to decide how to attain the desired goals. Choosing which options to implement establishes the direction the company will take. The budget reflects those decisions. As a manager at an ISP, for example, you may decide that, although the other two options are important, your

focus should be on maintaining state-of-the-art equipment to provide the most efficient service for your customers. Or, as manager of the baseball team, you could decide that raising prices would most effectively bring in the specified increase in revenues.

Coordinating and Communicating

Coordination is the act of gathering the pieces together—the individual unit budgets or division budgets—and balancing and combining them to achieve the master budget that expresses the organization's overall financial objectives and strategic goals. In many companies, this is quite a feat!

A master budget compiles the individual budgets from the functional areas of research and development, design, production, marketing, distribution, and customer service into one unit budget. Then the budgets from individual divisions, product lines, and subsidiaries are coordinated and integrated into a larger, cohesive result. Much like a composer weaving the music from many different instruments together to create a symphony, the master budget brings all the pieces together to achieve the organization's overall strategic plan and company mission. Details of the master budget will be discussed later in this chapter.

To achieve this end, communication is essential. Upper management needs to communicate the company's strategic objectives to all levels of the organization, and the individual planners need to communicate their particular needs, assumptions, expectations, and goals to those evaluating the departmental and functional budget pieces.

Additionally, the different groups within the company must always listen to one another. If one division is striving to achieve certain sales goals, then production must have that information to prepare for increased production capacity. If the company is introducing a new product, then the marketing department must be informed early in the planning process. The department will have to include in its budget the marketing efforts for the new product.

Monitoring Progress

Once the plan has been set in motion, the budget becomes a tool that managers can use to periodically monitor progress. They assess progress by comparing the actual results with the budgeted results. This feedback, or monitoring and evaluation of progress, in turn allows for timely corrective action. If, on the one hand, the interim evaluation shows that the organization is right on target, with actual results matching the budget's expected results, then no adjustment to the action plan is required. However, if you discover that the actual results are different from the expected results, then, simply put, you take corrective action. For example, if your baseball team's goal is to increase revenues 10 percent by raising prices, but you find after one month that the fans are resistant to higher prices, then you might take corrective action by offering bonus packages to offset the negative impact of the higher prices.

The difference between the actual results and the results expected by the budget is called a *variance*. A variance can be favorable, when the actual results are better than expected, or unfavorable, when the actual results are worse than expected. For example, after the first month of the new baseball season, you evaluate how the ticket sales are proceeding (table 7-1).

Overall, unit tickets sales are lower than expected, but you observe that there is a favorable variance for the higher-priced infield box seats (ticket buyers don't seem to mind the price hike for these seats). The biggest concern you have is the higher, unfavorable variance for the outfield grandstand seats. This is where you would concentrate your corrective action, because these fans seem to be responding to the higher prices by staying away. Thus, variance analysis can help you identify a problem early in the budget cycle and take the appropriate action.

Note here that we were strictly interested in units, not revenues. Managers could also conduct the budgeting exercise using revenues.

Evaluating Performance

Effective performance-evaluation systems contribute to the achievement of strategic goals, and budgets provide essential tools for meas-

TABLE 7-1

Ticket Sales Performance Report for April

| | AVERAGE TICKETS SOLD PER GAME | | |
	Actual Results	Budgeted Amounts	Variance
Infield Box	2,500	2,000	+ 500; favorable
Grandstand	6,850	7,000	– 150; unfavorable
Outfield Grandstand	7,700	9,000	– 1,300; unfavorable
Bleachers	11,850	12,000	– 150; unfavorable
Total	28,900	30,000	– 1,100; unfavorable

Source: HMM Budgeting.

uring management performance. After all, a manager who makes basic planning and implementation decisions should be held accountable for the results. By comparing the actual results to the budget for a given period, an evaluator can determine the manager's overall success in achieving his or her strategic goals. Performance evaluations serve a number of purposes:

- They motivate employees through reward systems based on performance.

- They provide the basis for compensation decisions, future assignments, and career advancement.

- They create a basis for future resource allocations.

Types of Budgets

The notion of the traditional budget has been under growing attack from those who believe that it no longer serves the needs of modern organizations. Critics complain that budgets are timed incorrectly (too long or too short), rely on inappropriate measures, and are

either too simplistic (or too complex), too rigid in a changing business environment, or too unchallenging (i.e., the bar is deliberately
set so that managers can hit their targets and collect their bonuses).
Many budgets we'll explore in this chapter were developed to address some of these difficult planning issues. But first, let's consider
different types of budgets.

Short–Term versus Long–Term Budgets

Budgets are typically developed to cover a one-year time span. But
the period covered by a budget may vary according to the purpose
of the budget, particularly as your company defines value creation. If
an organization is concerned with the profitability of a product over
its expected five-year life, then a five-year budget may be appropriate. If, on the other hand, a company is living hand-to-mouth, which
is the case with some start-up companies, then a month-by-month
budget that focuses on immediate cash flow might be more useful.

The length of the budget period may also depend on the type of
business. A pharmaceutical company, for example, is a relatively
stable business with a long-term planning horizon; here a longer-
term budget period would be expected. A dot-com start-up in the
volatile Internet universe, however, would have a much shorter time
frame for its budgeting process.

Fixed versus Rolling Budgets

A *fixed budget* covers a specific time frame—usually one fiscal year. At
the end of the year, a new budget is prepared for the following year.
A fixed budget may be reviewed at regular intervals—perhaps quarterly—so that adjustments and corrections can be made if needed,
but the basic budget remains the same throughout the period.

In an effort to address the problems of timeliness and rigidity in
a fixed budget, some firms, particularly those in rapid-change industries, have adopted a *rolling budget*. A rolling budget is a plan that is
continually updated so that the time frame remains stable while the
actual period covered by the budget changes. For example, as each

month passes, the one-year rolling budget is extended by one month, so that there is always a one-year budget in place. The advantage of a rolling budget is that managers have to rethink the process and make changes each month or each period. The result is usually a more accurate, up-to-date budget incorporating the most current information.

The disadvantage of a rolling budget is that the planning process can become too time-consuming. Moreover, if a company reviews its budget on a regular basis (say, every quarter for a one-year budget), analyzes significant variances, and takes whatever corrective action is necessary, then the fixed budget truly isn't as rigid as it seems.

Incremental versus Zero–Based Budgeting

Incremental budgeting extrapolates from historical figures. Managers look at the previous period's budget and actual results as well as expectations for the future in determining the budget for the next period. For example, a marketing department's budget would be based on the actual costs from the previous period but with increases for planned salary raises. The advantage of incremental budgeting is that history, experience, and future expectations are included in the development of the budget.

A disadvantage often cited by critics of the incremental budget is that managers may simply use the past period's figures as a base and increase them by a set percentage for the following budget cycle rather than taking the time to evaluate the realities of the current and future marketplace. Managers can also develop a use-it-or-lose-it point of view, with which managers feel they must use all the budgeted expenditures by the end of the period so that the following period's budget will not be reduced by the amount that would have been saved.

Zero-based budgeting describes a method that begins each new budgeting cycle from a zero base, or from the ground up, as though the budget were being prepared for the first time. Each budget cycle starts with a critical review of every assumption and proposed expenditure. The advantage of zero-based budgeting is that it requires managers to perform a much more in-depth analysis of each line item—considering objectives, exploring alternatives, and justifying their requests. The disadvantage of zero-based budgeting is that although it is more analytic and thorough, developing the budget can be extremely time-consuming, so much so that it may even interfere with actuating that budget. Planning needs to precede, but never overwhelm, action.

Kaizen Budgeting

Kaizen is a Japanese term that stands for continuous improvement, and *Kaizen budgeting* attempts to incorporate continuous improvement into the budgeting process. Cost reduction is built into the budget on an incremental basis so that continual efforts are made to reduce these costs over time. If the budgeted cost reductions are not achieved, then extra attention is given to that operating area. For example, a manufacturing plant may budget a continuous reduction in the cost of components, as shown below, putting pressure on suppliers to find further cost reductions.

January–February	$100.00
February–March	$99.50
March–April	$99.00

This type of incremental budgeting is difficult to maintain because the rate of budgeted cost reduction declines over time, making it more difficult to achieve improvements after the "easy" changes have been achieved.

The Master Budget

The *master budget* is the heart and soul of the budget. It brings all the pieces together, incorporating the operating budget and the financial budget of an organization into one comprehensive picture. In other words, the master budget summarizes all the individual financial projections within an organization for a given period.

For a typical for-profit organization, the operating budget consists of the budgets from functional areas—such as research and development, design, production, marketing, distribution, and customer service—and provides the budgeted income statement. The financial budget includes the capital budget, the cash budget, the budgeted balance sheet, and the budgeted cash flows. The master budget must integrate both the operating budget and the financial budget through an iterative process during which information flows back and forth from each element of the master budget (figure 7-1).

Master budgeting goes hand-in-hand with strategic planning at the highest level. Using the organization's strategic goals as its foundation, the budget-building process is both chronological and iterative, moving back and forth, testing assumptions and options.

Before preparing a master budget, senior managers must ask these three important questions:

1. Do the tactical plans being considered support the larger and longer-term strategic goals of the organization?

2. Does the organization have, or have access to, the required resources—that is, the cash it needs to fund the activities throughout the immediate budget period?

3. Will the organization create enough value to attract adequate future resources—profit, loans, investors, etc.—to achieve its longer-term goals?

Setting Assumptions

The first step in developing a budget is establishing a set of assumptions about the future. The assumptions that managers make will be directly affected by the answers to questions such as these:

- What are sales and marketing's expectations for unit sales and revenues from new and existing products?

- Are supplier prices anticipated to rise or fall?

- What will be the cost of the company's health-care plan for the coming year?

FIGURE 7-1

Master Budget Flow Chart

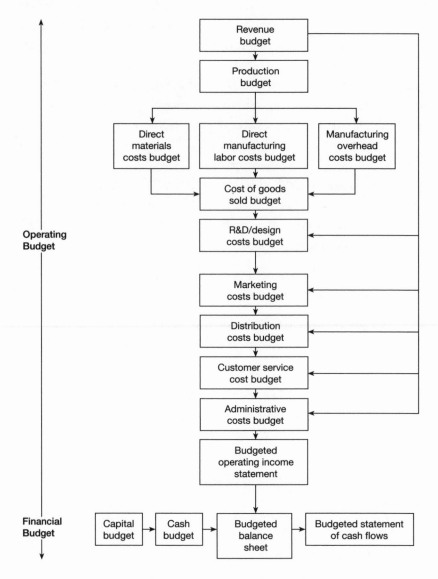

Source: HMM Budgeting. Adapted from Charles T. Horngren, George Foster, and Srikant M. Datar, *Cost Accounting* (New York: Prentice Hall, 2000).

Tips for Setting Assumptions

- Use historical data as a starting point. Even when times are changing quickly, information about past performance can establish a base from which to begin.

- Trust your own experience. Make educated guesses where necessary about what is likely to happen in the future.

- Listen to your intuition. Even though you can't verify those gut feelings, you can take them into account.

- Conduct due diligence. Seek out the information you need. This may involve doing research, reading trade journals, collecting industry statistics, and so on. And don't forget that the Internet is a growing information resource.

- Talk with and listen to knowledgeable people. Discuss your ideas with team members, colleagues, mentors. Seek out industry participants, suppliers, concerned community leaders, and experts in the field. Engage in discussions with competitors.

- Learn when to be a risk taker and when to be conservative. In a volatile market, conservative assumptions will be the safest.

- Test your assumptions. If possible, try out your assumptions in small experiments before you accept them.

- If the unemployment rate is expected to decline, will the company need to raise salaries to ensure an adequate work force in a tight labor market?

- What will competitors do to gain market share?

Assumptions should be sought from the sources that have the best information. For example, top management has a clear view of the strategic goals, and the finance group has records of past financial performance and future economic trends. Look to the human resources group for information on shifts in the labor market, and the sales representatives for the best information about sales prospects. Likewise, the purchasing department has the latest information about suppliers and price trends. Developing assumptions is a companywide endeavor in which communication and coordination play a key role.

Preparing the Operating Budget

An *operating budget* is nothing more than an agreed–upon pact between top management and other members of the management team. It is a target, not a forecast. It specifies revenues and costs for the coming period. These are expressed in a statement that resembles the income statement first described in chapter 1. The essential difference is that we are building the statement from expected versus actual quantities. In a nutshell, the operating budget is structured as follows:

Revenues − (Cost of Goods Sold + Sales, General, and Administrative Costs) = Operating Income

We have divided the operating budget process into five simple steps. For an interactive tool that will help you build and track your own operating budget, please visit www.elearning.hbsp.org/businesstools.

STEP 1: CALCULATE YOUR EXPECTED REVENUES. For the first step in preparing an operating budget, managers must apply some assumptions to forecast revenue growth (or decline). For our hypothetical for-profit company, Amalgamated Hat Rack, the managers of the Moose Head Division translate their assumptions about revenue growth based on past performance and future expectations of sales for their products during the fiscal year (table 7-3).

TABLE 7-2

Moose Head Division, Amalgamated Hat Rack, Year 1 Budget

	Prior Year's Actual	Year 1 Budget	Rate of Change
Sales by Model			
Moose Antler Deluxe	$201,000	$205,000	2.0%
Moose Antler Standard	$358,000	$381,000	6.4%
Standard upright	$515,500	$556,000	7.9%
Electro-revolving	$72,400	$60,250	(16.8%)
Hall/wall model	$81,200	$80,000	(1.5%)
Total sales	$1,228,100	$1,282,250	4.4%
Cost of Goods Sold			
Direct labor	$92,325	$96,500	4.5%
Factory overhead	$6,755	$7,200	7.0%
Direct materials	$211,000	$220,284	4.4%
Total cost of goods sold	$310,080	$323,984	4.5%
Marketing and Administrative Costs			
Sales salaries	$320,000	$331,200	3.5%
Advertising expenses	$145,000	$151,000	4.1%
Miscellaneous selling expenses	$4,200	$3,900	(7.1%)
Administrative expenses	$92,000	$94,500	2.7%
Total SG&A	$561,200	$580,600	3.46%
Operating Income	$355,820	$377,666	6.14%

Source: HMM Budgeting.

If they take an incremental-budgeting approach, the managers will use the prior year's actual sales of $1,228,100 as the base for developing their projections for the next year. If, on the other hand, they follow the zero-based budgeting method, they will make their sales projections for each model from the ground up, using fore-casted economic data, predicted consumer behavior, and other information. These will take recent experience with customer behavior, economic forecasts and other information into account.

Establishing projected revenue figures can create internal tensions. If managers are evaluated and rewarded on their achieving budgeted revenue targets, then they may be tempted to develop conservative revenue targets that will be easy to reach. This budgetary slack, or padding, provides a hedge for managers, making it more likely that actual revenues will be higher than budgeted revenues. With such results, the managers appear very effective.

Production constraints (the availability of qualified people for service firms and production capacity for manufacturers) may affect the revenue budget. If, for example, sales demand is expected to exceed the company's ability to manufacture and distribute, then the revenue budget is adjusted to match the production constraints rather than the actual demands of the market. Otherwise, the budget must add funds for building the capacity needed to meet demand.

STEP 2: CALCULATE THE EXPECTED COST OF GOODS SOLD. Once the revenue budget has been established, managers can then develop the budget for the cost of goods sold. The total number of units to be produced will form the basis for determining the direct costs, including labor and materials. In the same way, Moose Head Division calculates the indirect factory costs or overhead as part of the cost of goods sold budget. Remember here that sales are budgeted to rise 4.4 percent to $1,282,250.

STEP 3: CALCULATE THE OTHER EXPECTED COSTS. Other nonproduction costs include costs generated by research and development, product design, marketing, distribution, customer service, and administration. For Moose Head Division, with its classic hat rack designs, only various sales-related and administrative expenses make up the other-costs budget.

STEP 4: CALCULATE THE EXPECTED OPERATING INCOME. Finally, you can calculate the budgeted income statement. The difference between expected sales and expected costs results in the expected operating income. The managers of Moose Head Division provide their expected income statement to the top management of Amalgamated Hat Rack so that top management, in turn, can determine how Moose Head Division's budget fits with the company's master budget and overall strategic goals.

STEP 5: DEVELOP ALTERNATIVE SCENARIOS. Testing different scenarios is the "what if" iterative process of budgeting. How will a change in one area affect the expected outcome? What if we increase advertising? How much would that increase sales? What if the Moose Head employees decide to go on strike? How can we incorporate that risk into the budget?

For example, Amalgamated's management may decide to shift its strategic emphasis from increasing profits to developing a new product line in the Moose Head Division. Moose Head managers would then develop another set of budget figures indicating research and development costs that would reduce the current budgeted operating income. Alternatively, Moose Head managers could decide to accept bids from a new group of suppliers that would in turn reduce materials expenditures and increase the budgeted operating income.

Creating Financial Budgets

Once managers of operations have developed their operating budgets, or expected income statements, financial managers then plan for the capital required to support those operating budgets. You can't anticipate a 10 percent increase in sales, for example, without creating a parallel plan for the extra working capital and other inputs that will be required if the anticipated increase is realized. To plan for the requirements, managers need to develop three other budgets:

1. A cash budget that includes estimated cash from operations as well as other sources of cash (accounts payable, borrowing, or equity). The cash flow budget predicts and plans for the level and timing of cash inflow and outflow.

2. An operating asset investment plan that ensures that adequate capital will be available for operating assets such as inventory and accounts receivable

3. A capital investment plan that budgets for proposed investments in long-term productive assets such as property, plant,
and equipment expenditures and extended research-and-
development programs

These financial plans support the strategic objectives of the
organization, planning for both the near-term (cash budget) and the
long-term (capital investment plan) financial needs. They are
expressed in forecasted (or pro-forma) balance sheet and cash flow
statements to form a complete picture of the organization's expected
financial position during the budget period.

The *cash budget* is particularly important for the firm's financial
managers since it indicates shortages or surpluses of cash in each
period (usually months). No business can afford a shortfall of cash, as
the company would be unable to pay bills as they come due. The
cash budget shown in table 7-3 is one company's simplified cash
budget for a five-month period (January through May). Notice that
it identifies all cash inflows and outflows for each month. The ending cash balance of a given month becomes the beginning balance
for the next month. Thus, December's $220 ending balance becomes
January's beginning cash balance. By summing the monthly surplus
(or deficit) and the beginning cash balance, the budget finds the
ending balance for the month. A glance across the bottom line indicates when the enterprise will encounter a cash shortfall, as happens
here in April and becomes larger in May. Companies whose businesses are heavily seasonal—agricultural producers, garment makers,
ski manufacturers, and so forth—routinely experience wide swings
in ending cash balances.

During months of surplus, financial managers store company
cash in interest-bearing money market instruments such as short-
term bank certificates of deposit (CDs), commercial paper, and U.S.
Treasury bills. As surpluses disappear, they convert those instruments
back into cash and draw on lines of credit and short-term bank loans
to eliminate any cash deficits. As you can see in table 7-4, managers
must begin drawing on past surpluses in March. The surpluses have
evaporated by April, forcing them to seek outside sources of cash.

TABLE 7-3

A Simplified Cash Budget (in Thousands of Dollars)

	Dec.	Jan.	Feb.	March	April	May
Cash Inflows						
Sales revenues		1,100	875	600	500	600
Other revenues		250	225	200	200	0
Interest income			34	34	34	
Total inflows		1,350	1,134	834	734	600
Cash Outflows						
Purchases		400	380	320	300	350
Salaries		200	200	200	200	200
Hourly wages		170	165	150	195	220
Health-care payments		20	20	20	20	20
Retirement contributions		25	23	25	23	25
Interest payments		15	15	15	15	15
Taxes		305	295	270	260	240
Utilities		20	18	15	20	25
Total cash outflows		1,155	1,116	1,015	1,033	1,095
Cash Surplus or Deficit		195	18	(181)	(299)	(495)
Beginning Balance		220	415	433	252	(47)
Ending Balance	220	415	433	252	(47)	(542)

Seasonal and cyclical businesses use periods of heavy cash inflows to pay off their lines of credit and to build money market positions in anticipation of the next cash-consuming cycle.

Here are the steps to follow in building your own cash budget:

1. **Add receipts.** Determine the expected receipts—collections from customers and other sources—that will flow into the cash account each period. Cash collections may vary during the

budget period. For example, many retail stores expect to receive most of their receipts during holiday seasons.

2. **Deduct disbursements.** Based on expected activity, calculate how much cash will be required to cover disbursements—cash payouts—during the period. Disbursements could include payment for materials, payroll, taxes due, and so on. Some of these expenditures may be evenly distributed throughout the budget period, but some, such as payroll and materials costs, may fluctuate as part of the production process.

3. **Calculate the cash surplus or deficiency.** To calculate the cash surplus or deficiency for a period, subtract the disbursements from the sum of the beginning cash balance and the receipts expected during that period.

4. **Add the beginning cash balance.** The beginning cash balance is the ending balance from the previous period. By adding them together, you have a new ending balance.

5. **Determine financing needed.** The ending balance will be positive or negative. A positive balance indicates that you have more than enough cash to cover operations during that period. A negative balance indicates that the company must develop a plan for financing the shortfall from other sources, such as a bank loan. Repayment of any such loan must be reflected among the cash outflows of subsequent budget periods.

The Human Side of Budgeting

To some degree, preparing a budget is a matter of crunching numbers, a process being left more and more to financial modeling software, computers, and technology. But behind those numbers are real people like you—people who make assumptions, people who think about future situations, people who understand the idiosyncrasies of customers and competitors. Ideally, everyone involved in the budget process has the same goal in mind—achieving the organization's strategic objectives.

What some may see as a straightforward, even mechanical, process, however, is in reality complicated by genuine disagreements about assumptions of future trends and events, by conflicting functional needs, and by individual agendas that overshadow the larger corporate good. For this reason, the budget process can be defined as a series of negotiations between disparate interests. Top management wants the highest possible economic value in terms of profit. Middle management may have contrary needs, such as new equipment or new personnel. The human element is what can make the budget process so engaging and, at times, so frustrating.

Top-Down versus Participatory Budgeting

Top-down budgeting describes the process whereby upper management sets budget goals—revenue, profit, and so on—and imposes these goals on the rest of the organization. Thus, for example, the CEO of Amalgamated Hat Rack gives manager Claude Cervidés the goal of attaining an operating profit—or earnings before interest and taxes—of $400,000 for the upcoming fiscal year. It's then up to Claude to shape his operating budget with $400,000 as the operating profit target.

Top-down budgeting has many advantages. Since senior management has a clearer concept of the organization's strategic objectives, top-down budgeting assures the following benefits for senior management:

- Budget goals that reflect management's larger strategic objectives

- Better coordination of the budget requirements for all the elements of the organization

- The discouragement of "padding" managers' unit budgets

- High goals that challenge managers to stretch

Top-down budgeting has two main disadvantages. First, upper management may be out of touch with the realities of the individual divisions' production processes or markets. As a result, the goals they set may be inappropriate or unattainable. Second, middle managers may feel left out of the decision-making process and, consciously or unconsciously, may not fully participate in achieving the budgeted goals.

With participatory budgeting, the people responsible for achieving the budget goals are included in goal setting. Cervidés, for instance, would develop the budget for his own division, with the active participation of the heads of purchasing, human resources, production, marketing, and administration. Once his team had completed the budget, Cervidés would send it to Amalgamated Hat Rack's senior management. After review and possible feedback to Cervidés, they would incorporate this unit's budget, along with all the other budgets, into the master budget.

One advantage of participatory budgeting is that the people closest to the line activities—people who presumably have the best information—make the budget decisions. Also, participants in this type of budget process are more likely to make the extra effort to achieve the budgeted goals. The disadvantages of participatory budgeting are also twofold. First, the people closest to the line activities may not see the larger strategic picture. Second, if performance evaluations are tied to budget achievement, then the managers will have an incentive to pad their budgets either by underestimating revenues or by overestimating costs.

Iterative budgeting is an attempt to combine the best of both top-down and participatory budgeting. In the initial step, senior management provides the unit heads with a clear understanding of the organization's strategic goals. The unit heads then work with their teams to develop operating budgets that incorporate both their own tactical goals and the organization's larger strategic goals. After the unit heads send their budget proposals to upper management, upper management reviews the individual budgets and may ask for adjustments. And the negotiating process continues back and forth until a final master budget is achieved.

Tips for Negotiating Your Team's Budget

Effective budgeting requires a certain organizational savvy. Here are some tips for dealing with organizational issues that surround the budgeting process:

- Understand your organization's budgeting process. What are the guidelines you need to follow? What is the timing of the budget process? How is the budget used in the organization?

- Communicate often with the controller or finance person in your department. Ask questions about points you don't understand. Get that person's advice about the assumptions your team is making.

- Know what real concerns are driving the people making the decisions about your budget. Then be sure to address those concerns.

- Get buy-in from the decision makers. Spend time educating the finance person or decision maker about your area of the business. This will lay the groundwork for implementing changes later.

- Understand each line item in the budget you're working on. If you don't know what something means or where a number comes from, try to find out. Walk the floor. Talk to people on the line.

- Have an ongoing discussion with your team throughout the budget period. The more you plan, the more you will be able to respond to unplanned contingencies.

Avoid unpleasant surprises. As the numbers become available, compare actual figures to the budgeted amounts. If there is a significant or an unexpected variance, find out why. And be sure to notify the finance person who needs to know.

The key to success in any budgeting process is communication. Senior management has to communicate strategic goals in a way that makes sense. In turn, the unit heads communicate their resource needs and concerns when presenting budget proposals to management. All participants in the budget process have an obligation to listen to the various and sometimes conflicting positions.

Slack, Padding, and Sandbagging

Budgetary slack or padding occurs when managers believe they are going to be evaluated on their performance relative to the budget. To ensure that they will achieve their budgeted figures and be rewarded, they budget revenues conservatively or exaggerate anticipated costs, or do both. Both actions make the budget "game" easier to win. Budgetary slack also provides these managers with a hedge against unexpected problems, reducing the risk that groups will not "make their numbers." It's an old game that people from the top to the bottom learn to play.

Sandbagging is related to padding, but the misrepresentation can be something other than presenting lower-than-expected sales figures or higher costs. Sandbagging occurs when a manager conceals the true intent of a budgetary proposal. For example, Cervidés wants to aggressively expand the electro-revolving model of Amalgamated's Moose Head Division, but senior management has discouraged major investments in that project. So he may propose a minor investment in upgrading just the revolving mechanism in this budget cycle, knowing that he will broaden the upgrade into a much more ambitious redesign as a result of this "minor adjustment." This budgetary game is a form of sandbagging called the foot-in-the-door ploy.

What-If Scenarios and Sensitivity Analysis

Budgets are only as good as the future assumptions on which they are based. But assumptions are often wrong. We assume that customer A will purchase ten thousand units from us next year—and we have the sales agreement to back it up. But if customer A experiences a major business collapse, then that sales agreement isn't worth much. We assume that our energy bills will increase at roughly the current rate of inflation. But guess what? A cold winter and huge demand for energy may push prices through the roof.

Sensitivity analysis is an approach to dealing with assumptions and alternative options. As a budgetary tool, this analysis can greatly enhance the value of budgets as instruments for planning, feedback, and course correction. A sensitivity analysis applies a what-if situation to the budget model to see the effect of the potential change on the original data. For example, what if the cost of materials rises 5 percent, or what if sales rise 10 percent? Calculations for sensitivity analyses can be complicated when an analyst is dealing with a master budget that has summarized multiple divisional and/or functional budgets. Software packages for financial planning are available and commonly used to perform these calculations, giving managers a powerful tool to estimate the costs and benefits of various options and possibilities.

For example, if Moose Head Division wanted to test its assumptions with what-if scenarios, it could determine the effect of some likely alternative scenarios (table 7-4). Given the results of these analyses, Claude Cervidés may decide to direct his efforts toward lowering materials costs to achieve the best bottom-line result. Sensitivity analysis is discussed in more depth in chapter 9.

TABLE 7-4

Moose Head Division, Amalgamated Hat Rack, Sensitivity Analysis of Several Options

What-If Scenarios	Units Sold	Direct Materials Cost	Operating Income
Budget model	21,400	$214,000	$383,950
Scenario 1: increase unit sales 10%	23,540	$235,000	$422,730
Scenario 2: decrease unit sales 5%	20,330	$203,300	$360,900
Scenario 3: decrease materials cost 5%	21,400	$203,300	$398,700

Source: HMM Budgeting.

Tips for Effective Budgeting

If you want to use budgeting as a planning and team-building tool, you need to develop a game plan. Even if you recently finished this year's budget, it's not too early to start thinking about next year. In fact, doing so can make it more likely that your budget requests will be approved. Here are a few points to keep in mind.

- If you're a new manager, become familiar with your company's budgeting process.

- Spend time learning and understanding company priorities, as well as helping your team understand them.

- Make sure that any request for funds is in sync with the objectives set by senior management.

- Determine your unit's cost per output, however defined.

- Start gathering any information you will need, such as how your unit compares with other possible sources of the same product or service.

- Help team members begin learning about the budget. Ask for volunteers to research line items.

- Start by drafting a preliminary budget that estimates your costs and outputs. If they're not within the parameters set by management, look for ways to make adjustments.

- If you need to reduce costs, identify the activities that add value for the customer and those that don't. Analyze the cost of each, and begin by cutting non-value-added costs.

- Show how your budget request will generate income for the company. In other words, your budget should be not so much a request for funds as a proposal showing how you will help the company realize its goals.

Summing Up

This chapter began by describing the four basic functions of budgeting: planning, coordinating and communicating, monitoring progress, and evaluating performance. Together, these functions help an organization move forward and keep on track. And they make the time and trouble associated with budgeting worthwhile.

Several types of budgets, and their uses, were explained:

- Short–term versus long–term

- Fixed versus rolling

- Incremental versus zero–based

- Kaizen

- Master budget

The master budget brings together operating and cash budgets and various financial projections into a comprehensive picture. The steps for constructing operating and cash budgets were detailed.

Finally, the applications of what–if scenarios and sensitivity analysis were introduced. These methodologies can help budget makers predict the effects of specific changes in any important assumptions built in to the budget.

Note: If you'd like to get beyond the basics provided here, you can learn about activity-based budgeting (ABB) in this book's appendix. ABB is a new way of approaching the budgeting process using the activity-based costing concepts first introduced in chapter 3.

Practical Tools for Management Decisions

Making the Numbers Work for You

Key Topics Covered in This Chapter

- *Cost/benefit analysis*

- *Return on investment (ROI)*

- *Payback period*

- *Breakeven analysis*

- *Estimating nonquantifiable benefits and cost*

- *Tracking performance*

THE FIELD OF FINANCE and its accounting base of information provide a rich trove of practical tools that managers can use to assess business situations and to make decisions. These tools can help answer some of the most important questions that will ever come your way:

- What are the costs and benefits of a particular course of action?

- What is the estimated return on a potential investment?

- How long will it take for the company to recoup its investment in a particular project?

- How many units will the company have to sell at specific prices to simply break even on a venture?

- How can the company estimate nonquantifiable costs and benefits?

This chapter will show you how to answer these questions. It will also show you how to track the performance of an investment project undertaken in the wake of these forms of analysis.

Cost/Benefit Analysis

Amalgamated Hat Rack is considering two investment options: (1) buying a new piece of machinery and (2) creating a new product line. The new machine is a smart-technology, high-temperature plastic extruder costing $100,000. Amalgamated believes that this machinery will save time and money over the long term and is safer than the current machinery. The second option, launching a line of coat racks, will require a $250,000 investment in plant, equipment, and design. How can Amalgamated decide whether these investment options make economic sense?

The process of determining the answer is known as *cost/benefit analysis*. Basically, this form of analysis evaluates whether, over a given time frame, the benefits of the new investment, or the new business opportunity, outweigh the associated costs.

Before beginning any cost/benefit analysis, it's important to understand the cost of the status quo. You want to weigh the relative merits of each investment against the negative consequences, if any, of not proceeding with the investment. Cost/benefit analysis of a particular investment involves the following steps:

1. Identify the costs associated with the new purchase or business opportunity.

2. Identify the benefits of additional revenues that will result from the investment.

3. Identify the cost savings to be gained.

4. Map out the timeline for expected costs and anticipated revenues.

5. Evaluate the nonquantifiable benefits and costs—and there may be several.

The first three steps are fairly straightforward. Begin by identifying all the costs associated with the venture—this year's up-front costs as well as those you anticipate in subsequent years. Then consider the possible benefits. Additional revenues could come from more customers or from increased purchases by existing customers. To understand the benefits of these revenues, make sure to factor in the new costs associated with them; ultimately, this means you'll be looking at profit. With cost savings, it's a little simpler, at least in the sense that they represent incremental profit—they go straight to the bottom line. However, cost savings are sometimes more subtle and more difficult to recognize and quantify. These savings can arise from a variety of sources such as these improvements:

- **More efficient processing.** This could mean that fewer people are required to do the same work, or that the process requires fewer steps, or even that the time spent on each step decreases.

- **More accurate processing.** Both the time required to correct errors and the number of lost customers could decrease. The "scrap" rate—i.e., the rate at which a manufacturing process produces unsalable output—may also go down.

Next, map out the costs and the revenues—or cost savings—over the relevant period. When do you expect the costs to be incurred? In what increments? When do you expect to receive the benefits (additional revenues or cost savings)? In what increments? Once that's done, you're ready to begin the evaluation phase using one or more of the analytical tools subsequently covered in this chapter: accounting return on investment, payback period, and breakeven analysis.

Accounting Return on Investment

As discussed earlier, return on investment (ROI)—or, to use the more technical term, accounting return on investment—is not always the best measure of the success of an investment. But because many managers still use ROI, it pays to understand how they look at it. Accounting return on investment (ROI) can take the form of cost savings, incremental profit, or value appreciation. You begin by determining the net return. To calculate the net return from an investment, subtract the total cost of the investment from the total benefits received. Then, to calculate the ROI, divide the net dollar amount of return by the total cost of investment.

Let's suppose that the new $100,000 extruder Amalgamated is considering would realize an annual $18,000 savings for the company over the lifetime of the machine, which is estimated to be seven years. The total savings would thus be $126,000 ($18,000 × 7), making for a net return of $26,000 ($126,000 − $100,000). Applying the formula for ROI—that is, net return divided by total cost of investment, or $26,000 divided by $100,000 in this example—the ROI is 26 percent.

Is 26 percent a good return? In isolation, the figure has no particular meaning, since ROI is a way of comparing returns on money a company invests internally with returns available to it elsewhere at the *same level of risk*. The notion of equal risk is very important here, since all investors demand higher returns for higher risk. Thus, it makes no sense to compare the returns the company believes it could make from an investment in A, the relatively safe expansion of a current product line, with an investment in B, a totally new product line for an untested market. The risk levels of the two potential investments are simply not equivalent. The higher-risk investment should have a higher potential return.

ROI as described in this example is also flawed because it ignores the time value of money, a core financial concept covered later in the book. For example, which would you rather have (assuming equal risks), an investment that gave you a 26 percent return in one year, or an investment that gave you the same return at the end of seven years? No contest there. Any rational investor would want the money sooner than later.

Thus, the utility of ROI as a decision-making tool is rather limited. Nevertheless, since many businesspeople use ROI, it pays to understand the measurement and its weaknesses.

Payback Period

Companies also want to know the *payback period*: how long it will take a particular investment to pay for itself. We already know that the plastic extruder is expected to save Amalgamated $18,000 a year. To determine the payback period, divide the total amount of the investment by the annual savings expected. In this case, $100,000 divided by $18,000 equals 5.56. In other words, the extruder will pay for itself in 5.56 years. Table 8-1 below provides a year-by-year illustration of how annual savings will accumulate.

Note that Amalgamated will not truly begin to reap the benefits of the investment for more than five years. But what if the life-span estimates are wrong, and the extruder wears out after four years? The investment now appears to be not particularly attractive—certainly less attractive than an investment with a similar ROI and a payback period of three years.

As an analytical tool, the payback period tells you only one thing: how long it will take to recoup your investment. Although it is not useful in comparing real alternatives, some executives still rely on it.

Breakeven Analysis

Breakeven analysis tells you how much (or how much more) you need to sell in order to pay for the fixed investment—in other

TABLE 8-1

Amalgamated Hat Rack, Cumulative Annual Savings from the Installment of a Plastic Extruder

Year	Savings	Cumulative Savings
1	$18,000	$18,000
2	$18,000	$36,000
3	$18,000	$54,000
4	$18,000	$72,000
5	$18,000	$90,000
6	$18,000	$108,000
7	$18,000	$126,000

Source: HMM Finance.

words, at what point you will break even on your cash flow. With that information in hand, you can look at market demand and competitors' market shares to determine whether it's realistic to expect to sell that much. Breakeven analysis can also help you think through the impact of changing price and volume relationships.

More specifically, the breakeven calculation helps you determine the volume level at which the total after-tax contribution from a product line or an investment covers its total fixed costs. But before you can perform the calculation, you need to understand the components that go into it:

- **Fixed costs.** These are costs that stay mostly the same, no matter how many units of a product or service are sold—costs such as insurance, management salaries, and rent or lease payments. For example, the rent on the production facility will be the same, whether the company makes ten thousand or twenty thousand units, and so will the insurance.

- **Variable costs.** Variable costs are those that change with the number of units produced and sold; examples include utilities, labor, and the costs of raw materials. The more units you make, the more you consume these items.

- **Contribution margin.** This is the amount of money that every sold unit contributes to paying for fixed costs. As described in chapter 3, it is defined as net unit revenue minus variable (or direct) costs per unit.

With these concepts understood, we can make the calculation. We are looking for the solution to this straightforward equation:

Breakeven Volume = Fixed Costs / Unit Contribution Margin

And here's how we do it. First, find the unit contribution margin by subtracting the variable costs per unit from the net revenue per unit. Then divide total fixed costs, or the amount of the investment, by the unit contribution margin. The quotient is the breakeven volume, that is, the number of units that must be sold in order for all fixed costs to be covered.

To see breakeven analysis in practice, let's look again at the plastic extruder example. Suppose that each hat rack produced by the extruder sells for $75, and that the variable cost per unit is $22. Then

$75 (Price per Unit) − $22 (Variable Cost per Unit) = $53 (Unit Contribution Margin)

therefore

$100,000 (Total Investment Required) / $53 (Unit Contribution Margin) = 1,887 Units

The preceding calculations indicate that Amalgamated must sell 1,887 hat racks to recover its $100,000 investment.

At this point, Amalgamated must decide whether the breakeven volume is achievable: Is it realistic to expect to sell 1,887 additional hat racks, and if so, how quickly?

A Breakeven Complication

Our hat rack breakeven analysis represents a simple case. It assumes that costs are distinctly fixed or variable, that costs and unit contributions will not change as a function of volume (i.e., that the sale price of the item under consideration will not change at different levels of output). These assumptions may not hold in your more complicated world. Rent may be fixed up to a certain level of production, then increase by 50 percent as you rent a secondary facility to handle expanded output. Labor costs may in reality be a hybrid of fixed and variable. And as you push more and more of your product into the market, you may find it necessary to offer price discounts—which reduces contribution per unit. You will need to adjust the breakeven calculation to accommodate these untidy realities.

Operating Leverage

Your goal as a businessperson, of course, is not to break even but to make a profit. Once you've covered all your fixed costs with the contributions of many unit sales, every subsequent sale contributes directly to profits. As we observed above,

Unit Net Revenue − Unit Variable Cost = Unit Contribution to Profit

You can see at a glance that the lower the unit variable cost, the greater the contribution to profits will be. In the pharmaceutical business, for example, the unit cost of cranking out and packaging a bottle of a new wonder drug may be less than a dollar. Yet if the company can sell each bottle for $100, a whopping sum of $99 contributes to corporate profits once sales have gotten beyond the breakeven point! The trouble is that the pharmaceutical company may have invested $400 million up front in fixed product development costs just to get the first bottle out the door. It will have to sell many bottles of the new medication just to break even. But once it does, profits can be extraordinary.

The relationship between fixed and variable costs is often described in terms of *operating leverage*. Companies whose fixed costs are high relative to their variable costs are said to have high operating leverage. The pharmaceutical business, for example, generally operates with high operating leverage. So too does the software industry—the greater percentage of its costs are fixed product development outlays; the variable cost of the CDs on which programs are distributed represent only pennies.

Now consider the opposite: *low* operating leverage. Here fixed costs are low relative to the total cost of producing every unit of output. A law firm is a good example of low operating leverage. The firm has a minimal investment in equipment and fixed expenses. The bulk of its costs are the fees it pays its attorneys, which vary depending on the actual hours they bill to clients.

Operating leverage is a great thing once a company passes its breakeven point, but it can cause substantial losses if breakeven is never achieved. In other words, it's risky. This is why managers give so much thought to finding the right balance between fixed and variable costs.

Estimating Nonquantifiable Benefits and Costs

Because the numbers seldom tell the whole story, your cost/benefit, breakeven, and other forms of analysis must often incorporate qualitative factors as well. Examples here include the strategic fit of the new opportunity with the company's mission, the ability to take on the new opportunity without losing focus, the likelihood of success given market conditions, and perhaps an increase in customer goodwill that the new investment would bring about.

Even though such factors are not fully quantifiable, try to quantify them as much as possible. Make assumptions that can help you come up with a ballpark figure. Suppose you're trying to assess the value of improved information—more comprehensive data that is easier to understand and more widely available—that a new investment would bring. You could try to come up with a dollar figure that represents the value of employees' time saved by the new information, or the value of the increased customer retention that might be gleaned from your better understanding of purchase patterns. Such estimates should not necessarily be incorporated into your ROI or other quantified analysis, but they can be very persuasive nevertheless.

Weigh the quantifiable and the nonquantifiable factors. For example, if an investment opportunity is only marginally positive, you may want to give equal weight to more qualitative considerations such as strategic fit in your final decision.

Tracking Performance

Once you've decided to undertake an investment opportunity, you should monitor its progress, checking to assure that ongoing results and earlier projections are on course. Track your projections against

TABLE 8-2

Amalgamated Hat Rack, Coat Rack Division, January 2002 Budget

	Budget Jan.	Actual Jan.	Variance
Coat Rack Revenues	$39,000	$38,725	-275
Cost of Goods Sold	$19,500	$19,200	-300
Gross Margin	$19,500	$19,525	+25
Marketing Expense	$8,500	$10,100	+1,600
Administrative Expense	$4,750	$4,320	-430
Total Operating Expense	$13,250	$14,420	+1,170
Operating Profit (EBIT)	$6,250	$5,105	-1,145

Source: HMM Finance.

actual revenues and expenses. It's a good idea to do this on a monthly basis, so that you can spot potential problems early on. With that in mind, let's revisit the projections for the new coat rack division at Amalgamated Hat Rack. Table 8-2 shows the state of affairs early in the first quarter.

The division is doing reasonably on revenues and cost of goods sold. Its only really large negative variance is in the marketing expense line. Because the numbers are based on just the first month's figures, it is difficult to know if the variance is simply a onetime, or seasonal, variation or if Amalgamated is going to have to spend more on marketing than anticipated. If your investment is not tracking according to budget, and if it looks as if the pattern of unexpectedly high costs (or unexpectedly low revenues) is going to hold, then you may need to rethink the initiative—or even to discontinue it.

Summing Up

Finance and accounting concepts can help managers make better decisions. This chapter has described several:

- Cost/benefit analysis

- Accounting return on investment

- Payback period—a way to estimate the number of months or years required to recoup your initial investment

- Breakeven analysis, which tells you how much (or how much more) you need to sell in order to pay for the fixed costs.

The chapter has also shown how you can deal with nonquantitative cost/benefit factors and track investment performance. Understanding these concepts, and their limitations, can help you do your job more effectively.

9

The Time Value of Money

Calculating the Real Value of Your Investment

Key Topics Covered in This Chapter

- *Present and future value*

- *Net present value*

- *Internal rate of return*

- *Hurdle rate, discount rate, and the cost of capital*

- *Economic value added*

I N CHAPTER 8, WE EXAMINED return on investment (ROI) and payback period analysis—two tools that managers use to make decisions and assess performance. We noted, however, that these have one important weakness: They fail to account for the time value of money. That is, though they indicate (or estimate) inflows and outflows of cash, ROI and payback analysis fail to recognize *when* those cash flows take place. As we'll explain here, the timing of those cash flows matters, and should be factored into management decisions.

This chapter will introduce you to financial decision-making tools that account for time value: specifically, present and future value, net present value, and internal rate of return. You will also become acquainted with associated concepts that you're likely to encounter when management discusses serious long-term investments—hurdle rate, discount rate, and the company's cost of capital. The chapter also includes a discussion of sensitivity analysis, a method that increases the practicality of these time-value tools.

What Is Time Value?

The time value of money is a mathematically based recognition that money received today is worth more than an equal amount of money received months or years in the future. If you have any doubts about this statement, consider the following example:

> *Your father-in-law takes you aside and says, "The grim reaper is going to catch up with me one of these days. And as much as I'd like to take all of my money with me, I've decided to give you youngsters a bundle of it before I go—say, three hundred thousand dollars."*

Naturally, you're pleased to learn of his generous intention. You are also eager to learn *when* the money will be coming your way. "I'm not sure when I'll give you the money," he continues. "It might be this year, next year, or five years down the road. But that shouldn't matter since it will be three hundred thousand in any case."

Your father-in-law got that last point dead wrong. *When* you receive the money does matter. Thanks to the effect of compounding interest, $300,000 put today into a bank CD or savings account with a 5 percent annual interest rate would be worth almost $383,000 five years from now—and slightly more than $483,000 if your investment compounded at a 10 percent annual rate! Let's look at how compounding works over time using the $300,000 in our example, with annual compound interest at 10 percent per year over five years (table 9-1).

TABLE 9-1

Time Value of an Investment with 10 Percent Compounded Interest

Period	Beginning Value	Interest Earned	Ending Value
1	$300,000	+ $30,000	$330,000
2	$330,000	+ $33,000	$363,000
3	$363,000	+ $36,300	$399,300
4	$399,300	+ $39,930	$439,230
5	$439,230	+ $39,930	$483,153

This example demonstrates the importance of time in the receipt of cash amounts. If your father-in-law were to give you the $300,000 today, you'd be $183,153 better off (assuming a 10 percent compounded return) than if he delayed his gift to you by five years. (Note: This analysis assumes that you reinvest the interest you earn at the same rate.)

The example also introduces a number of important terms in the language of finance. The $300,000 is a present value (PV), that is, an amount received today. The $483,153 is a *future value* (FV)—the amount to which a present value, or series of payments, will increase over a specific period at a specific compounding rate. The number of periods (n) in this example is five years. And the rate (i) is 10 percent. Understand these terms, and you'll probably rise a notch or two in the estimation of your company's CFO.

Generations of business students have been forced to learn how to calculate time values using tables like the one in table 9-2. This table indicates the future value of $1, given various compounding rates and compounding periods. Each cell in the table is commonly referred to as a future value interest factor, or FVIF. Tables such as these are easy to use.

The table shows that the FVIF for five periods at 10 percent is 1.6105. Considering the example of the father-in-law's $300,000 gift, we can now find the future value of $300,000 after five years at a 10 percent annual interest rate. To do so, we follow this simple formula:

Present Value × FVIF = Future Value

$300,000 × 1.6105 = $483,150

This amount is the future value we found earlier using a long-handed method (with a slight difference due to rounding).

Every finance text has an appendix of tables that you can used to solve time-value problems. But thanks to today's preprogrammed business calculators and electronic spreadsheets, you don't need them. A business calculator like the ubiquitous Hewlett-Packard

TABLE 9-2

Future Value of $1 (FVIF)

Periods	8%	9%	10%	11%	12%
1	1.0800	1.0900	1.1000	1.1100	1.1200
2	1.1664	1.1881	1.2100	1.2321	1.2544
3	1.2597	1.2950	1.3310	1.3676	1.4049
4	1.3605	1.4116	1.4641	1.5181	1.5735
5	1.4693	1.5386	1.6105	1.6851	1.7623
6	1.5869	1.6771	1.7716	1.8704	1.9738
7	1.7138	1.8280	1.9487	2.0762	2.2107
8	1.8509	1.9926	2.1436	2.3045	2.4760
9	1.9990	2.1719	2.3579	2.5580	2.7731
10	2.1589	2.3674	2.5937	2.8394	3.1058
11	2.3316	2.5804	2.8531	3.1518	3.4786
12	2.5182	2.8127	3.1384	3.4985	3.8960

12C has several keys programmed to make these solutions simple. Its keyboard has keys for present value (PV), future value (FV), compounding rate (i), and number of compounding periods (n). If you know any three of these variables, the calculator will solve for the fourth. The instruction book explains the sequence to follow in entering the values and obtaining the solution. Likewise, PC spreadsheet programs such as Microsoft's Excel have built-in formulas that make time-value problems easy to solve.

Net Present Value

Future value is an easy idea to grasp, since most of us have been exposed to the principle of compound interest. Put money in an interest-bearing account, leave it alone, and it will grow to a larger amount over time. The longer you leave it alone, or the higher the compounding rate, or both, the larger the future value. The idea of the present value of a future sum is less familiar and less intuitive, but financial people and other savvy managers use it all the time. You can too.

Present value is the monetary value today of a future payment discounted at some annual compound interest rate. To understand the concept of present value, let's go back to our initial example—the bequest from your father-in-law. In that example, the present value of $483,153 is $300,000. This is calculated through a process of discounting, or reverse compounding, at a rate of 10 percent per year over a period of five years. In the parlance of finance, 10 percent is the *discount rate*. If your father-in-law had said, "Look, I'm planning on giving you $483,153 five years from now, but if you'd rather have the money today I'm willing to give you $300,000," he'd be giving you an equivalent value, assuming you could invest it at 10 percent annually. In short, you would be indifferent between getting $300,000 now or $483,153 in five years—unless you worried about your father-in-law's not making good on his promise.

As with future value, tables are available for calculating the present value of $1 received in the future. Table 9-3 indicates the present-value interest factors (PVIFs) for $1 received in the future within a range of discount rates and discounting periods.

Note that the PVIF for five periods at 10 percent is 0.621. We can use this factor to calculate the present value of your father-in-law's $483,153 gift received five years in the future:

Future Value × PVIF = Present Value

$483,153 × 0.621 = $300,038

We're off by just a little as a result of rounding of the PVIF in the table.

The PVIF table clearly indicates how the present value of money received in the future shrinks with time. Scan any discount rate column in the PVIF table from top to bottom. The first number

TABLE 9-3

Present Value of $1 (PVIF)

Period	2%	4%	6%	8%	10%	12%
1	0.980	0.962	0.943	0.926	0.909	0.893
2	0.961	0.925	0.890	0.857	0.826	0.797
3	0.942	0.889	0.840	0.794	0.751	0.712
4	0.924	0.855	0.792	0.735	0.683	0.636
5	0.906	0.822	0.747	0.681	0.621	0.567
6	0.888	0.790	0.705	0.630	0.564	0.507
7	0.871	0.760	0.665	0.583	0.513	0.452
8	0.853	0.731	0.627	0.540	0.467	0.404
9	0.837	0.703	0.592	0.500	0.424	0.361
10	0.820	0.676	0.558	0.463	0.386	0.322

is the value of $1 received a year from now. In the 10 percent column, that value is $0.91. The same dollar is worth only $0.39 if you must wait ten years to get your hands on it. Strictly chump change. Notice, too, the role that the discount rate plays in shrinking future values over time. At 6 percent, $1 received ten years from now is worth $0.59. But at a discount rate of 12 percent, that same dollar is down to a mere $0.32! Thus, present value "shrinkage" has two sources: time and the discount rate. The greater the time and the higher the rate, the less your future cash flows will be worth.

Your financial calculator and PC spreadsheet can handle this same calculation. You simply enter the known values (future value, discount rate, and number of compounding periods) and solve for the unknown value, PV.

Now that you understand present value, let's move on to a typical business situation and see how time-value calculations can help your decision making. But first let's broaden the concept of present value to *net present value* (NPV), which is the present value of one or more future cash flows *less* any initial investment costs. To illustrate this concept, let's say that Amalgamated Hat Rack expects its new product line to start generating $70,000 in annual profit (or, more specifically, net cash flows) beginning one year from now. For simplicity, we'll also say that this level of annual profit will continue for the succeeding five years (totaling $350,000). Bringing the product line on stream will require an up-front investment of $250,00. The questions for the company can thus be phrased as follows: Given this expected profit stream and the $250,000 up-front cost required to produce it, is a new line of coat racks the most productive way to invest that initial $250,000? Or would Amalgamated be better off investing it in something else?

A net-present-value calculation answers this question by recognizing that the $350,000 in profit that Amalgamated expects to receive over five years is not worth $350,000 in current dollars. Because of the time value of money, it is worth less than that. In other words, that future sum of $350,000 has to be discounted back into an equivalent of today's dollars. How much it is discounted depends on the rate of return Amalgamated could reasonably expect to receive had it chosen to put the initial $250,000 investment into something other than the line of coat racks (but similar in risk) for the same period. As explained earlier, this rate of return is often called the discount rate. We define the discount rate as the annual rate, expressed as a percentage, at which a future payment or series of payments is reduced to its present value. In our Amalgamated example, let's assume a discount rate of 10 percent. But before we describe the calculation, let's lay out the situation as follows, with the values in thousands of dollars:

Year	0	1	2	3	4	5
Cash flows	−250	+70	+70	+70	+70	+70

Here we see a negative cash flow of $250,000 in year zero, the starting point of our investment project. This is the cash outflow required to get the project off the ground. The company then experiences a positive cash flow of $70,000 *at the end* of each of the next five years.

Beginning or End of the Period

In solving for net present value and other time-value problems, it is important to know if the cash flows take place at the beginning or end of the period. The present value of a cash flow received in early January is worth more than the same amount received in late December of the same year. Your financial calculator and electronic spreadsheet are set up to accommodate this important difference.

To find the net present value of Amalgamated's stream of cash flows, we need to find the present value of each of the $70,000 cash flows, discounted at 10 percent for the appropriate number of years. If we add together the present values of the five annual inflows and then subtract the $250,000 initially invested, we will have the NPV of the investment. We can determine the NPV for this set of cash flows using our PVIF table in exhibit 9-4 and its present-value interest factors.[1]

Calculations such as this one can be laborious, but the financial calculators and computer spreadsheets now available make them faster and more accurate. All that you have to do is plug in the right

TABLE 9-4

Net Present Value of Amalgamated's Cash Flow

	Cash Flows (in $1,000)	PVIF	PV (in $1,000)
Year 0	− 250		− 250.00
Year 1	+ 70	0.909	+ 63.63
Year 2	+ 70	0.826	+ 57.82
Year 3	+ 70	0.751	+ 52.57
Year 4	+ 70	0.683	+ 47.81
Year 5	+ 70	0.621	+ 43.47
Total			+ 15.30

numbers in the right sequence. The NPV function on your calculator or spreadsheet takes into consideration your initial investment,
each periodic cash flow, your discount rate, and the number of years
over which you will receive the cash flows.

If the resulting NPV is a positive number, and no other investments are under consideration, then the investment should be pursued. In the Amalgamated case depicted in table 9-4, the NPV for
the line of coat racks is a positive $15,300, which suggests that it
would be an attractive investment for Amalgamated.[2] Its compound
annual return is at least 10 percent.

But what about the other investment Amalgamated is considering, the $100,000 plastic extruder described in chapter 8? Let's
reanalyze that investment option through the lens of NPV. As mentioned, the company was considering spending $100,000 to pur-
chase and install a new extruder that, according to its best estimates,
would save $18,000 each year over the seven-year lifetime of the
machine. We can set up the problem as follows, with cash flows in
thousands of dollars:

Year	0	1	2	3	4	5	6	7
Cash flows	−100	+18	+18	+18	+18	+18	+18	+18

At a discount rate of 10 percent, and using the PVIF table in
table 9-2, we determine that the NPV of the extruder project
is −$12,368. As a negative NPV, it probably shouldn't be pursued.

Here we should emphasize the effect that the discount rate has
on NPV. The greater the discount rate, the lower the present value of
future cash flows. Suppose that Amalgamated's discount rate were 6
percent instead of 10 percent. In that case, the NPV for the extruder
would be slightly positive.

Notice something else about the NPV calculation for the
extruder. Even with a 6 percent discount rate, the NPV is far less
positive than the rosy 26 percent return on investment (ROI) we calculated in chapter 8. That ROI represented 26 per-cent over a seven-
year period but failed to account for the time value of money. As a
decision tool, ROI has very limited value. NPV analysis provides a
more precise evaluation of investment opportunities.

Complications

Of course, business situations are almost always more complex than the conveniently simple ones we've contrived in the Amalgamated examples. Project investments are rarely made in a single lump sum at the very beginning, and cash flows are almost always irregular—some positive, others negative—over time. What's more, it is often difficult or impossible to accurately estimate what cash flows will look like far in the future, or when they will finally end. Some investments end abruptly with the sale of the product line or factory building—the net sale value of which must be entered as a terminal-value cash flow. Other investments may go on for decades and gradually fade to nothing.

With this complexity in mind, we will try to present a slightly more realistic picture of a business using NPV analysis. Let's deliberately make Amalgamated's new product line investment project slightly more complex. We'll do this in three ways and then show how you could assess the investment project through the same NVP analysis framework:

1. We'll spread the $250,000 investment over three periods instead of one. This is more typical of business practice in developing a new product line.

2. Cash flows will be made more irregular, with a loss in the first full year and growing profitability in later years.

3. We'll arbitrarily plan for Amalgamated to sell the product line at the end of five years for $170,000, and we'll treat the sale price as a terminal value.

Table 9-5 shows the results of these assumptions. Using 10 percent as the discount rate, we calculate a NPV of about $69,800 for this series of negative and positive cash flows. If 10 percent is the cost of capital to Amalgamated, we could say that this investment would (1) earn its cost of capital *and* (2) make a positive present-value contribution of $69,800.

TABLE 9-5

Net Present Value of Amalgamated's Cash Flow, with Complications (Values in Thousands)

	YEAR					
	0	**1**	**2**	**3**	**4**	**5**
Cash Investments	− 150	− 75	− 25	0	0	0
Cash Flow from Operations		− 15	+ 40	+ 80	+ 90	+ 100
Terminal Value						+ 170
Net Cash Flow	− 150	− 90	+ 15	+ 80	+ 90	+ 270
PVIF		0.909	0.826	0.751	0.683	0.621
PV	− 150	− 81.81	+ 12.39	+ 60.08	+ 61.47	+ 167.67
NPV	+ 69.80					

More Complications

Our presentation makes NPV analysis seem as straightforward as the mathematics on which it rests. It is straightforward, but the cash flows we use are, unfortunately, merely estimates. Consider Amalgamated's $250,000 investment. Where did that number come from? Chances are it is an agreed-upon estimate produced by people in Amalgamated's research and development and manufacturing units. Those people have experience in designing new products and setting up the manufacturing equipment needed to crank them out. But past experience is an uncertain guide to the future. The only thing that you can say with certainty is that the cost of the investment will be more or less than $250,000!

Estimates of the net cash flows from operations are bound to be even less certain. Consider how cash flow from operations is determined. The product line manager no doubt asks the marketing department three questions:

1. How many of these new products (in units) can your people sell in each of the next five years?

2. What would be our net revenues from each sale?

3. What level of marketing budget would you need to achieve those sales at those prices?

The manager would likewise get a unit production and labor and materials cost estimate from the manufacturing unit. In effect, the new-product manager would have to develop a detailed "mini" income statement similar to the enterprise income statement described in chapter 1. This statement would detail the revenues and costs (i.e., materials, labor, marketing, and all other costs) associated with the new product line over the five-year span of the analysis. The sum of the revenues and costs would be the cash flow from operations.

Taken together, these annual estimated cash flows from operations would be used in determining the NPV of the project. Obviously, there are lots of assumptions here, and plenty of room for error—especially as people attempt to forecast sales further and further into the future. There is even a chance that sales of the new product line will cannibalize the sales of existing product lines. As a consequence, opponents of the particular investment can usually find lots of opportunities to take potshots at the numbers, and experienced decision makers usually insist on fairly conservative sales forecasts and cost estimates.

Nevertheless, careful NPV analysis based on sound assumptions is an excellent decision-making tool—and it's certainly better than the alternatives. Its value can be improved if the NPV of an investment is presented in worst-case, most-likely-case, and best-case scenarios. This approach captures a broader range of opinions in the organization about future unit sales, various costs of production, and other assumptions.

Case Study: Beyond NVP

Farnsworth Dabble, vice president of product development for Amalgamated Hat Rack, was just wrapping up his presentation of the new-product-line proposal to senior management. He directed his audience's attention to the five-year series of cash flows that he and his colleagues anticipated from the proposed new product line. "And so you see that we anticipate negative cash flows in each of the first two years of the project, mostly due to R&D expenditures and production ramp-up. But over the next three years, we anticipate healthy cash flows, particularly if we sell the product line and its production facilities at the end of year five."

Dabble went on to explain the assumptions made in determining those cash flows, the internal debates underlying them, and his team's wish to err on the side of conservative projections. "As you can see," he concluded with satisfaction, "the proposed product line has a positive net present value."

The CFO was the first to respond. "So, what's the internal rate of return for this project?"

Dabble stiffened. Internal rate of return? He'd heard that term used before and had a sense of its meaning, but he was clueless about how to do the actual calculation or respond to the CFO's question. In the end, he was forced to utter the three dreaded words, hoping that none of his underlings were within earshot: "I don't know."

Internal Rate of Return

The *internal rate of return* (IRR) is another tool that managers can use to decide whether to commit to a particular investment opportunity, or to rank the desirability of various opportunities. IRR is defined as the discount rate at which the NPV of an investment equals zero. Let's consider what that means in terms of our more complicated version of Amalgamated's cash flow projection for its new product line:

Year	0	1	2	3	4	5
Net cash flow	−150	-90	+15	+80	+90	+270

As calculated earlier, the NPV of this stream of cash flows discounted at 10 percent was a positive $69,800. That told us that these numbers, if realized, would cover Amalgamated's cost of capital (10 percent) *and* contribute an additional present value of $69,800. IRR tells us something more. It captures the discount rate *and* the additional present value contribution in a single number. To calculate it, we need to determine the discount rate that would reduce NPV to exactly zero. IRR is that discount rate.

We know right off the bat that the IRR for our example must be greater than 10 percent since the cash flow discounted at 10 percent produced a positive NPV. But how much more? Well, if we had a few blackboards and several hours, we could calculate the IRR through an iterative process that used higher and higher discount rates. Eventually, we'd get to the one that produced an NPV of zero. But financial calculators and electronic spreadsheets again come to the rescue, making IRR calculations very easy. All we need to do is enter the values for each of the cash flows and solve for the discount rate (i). The IRR calculation is based on the same algebraic formula as the NPV calculation. With the NPV calculation, you know the discount rate, or the desired rate or return, and are solving the equation for the NPV of the future cash flows. In contrast, with IRR, the NPV is set at zero and the discount rate is unknown. The equation solves for the discount rate. For the Amalgamated project just described, the IRR is about 17.7 percent.

Typically, when the IRR is greater than the opportunity cost (the expected return on a comparable investment) of the capital required, the investment under consideration should be undertaken. You can use your company's *hurdle rate* as the IRR target. The CFO usually prescribes the hurdle rate. The hurdle rate is a minimal rate of return that all investments for a particular enterprise must achieve. The IRR of the investment under consideration must exceed the hurdle rate in order for the company to go forward with it.

Hurdle Rate and the Cost of Capital

We have defined the hurdle rate as the minimal rate of return that all investments for a particular enterprise must achieve. The firm's *cost of capital* is more specific. It is the weighted average cost of the organization's different sources of capital: both debt and equity.

Everyone understands that the debt capital employed by corporations has a cost—namely, the interest paid on bonds and other IOUs. But few nonfinancial people think of the capital contributed by owners as having a real cost. But it does. This cost is an opportunity cost—what the shareholders could earn on their capital if they invested in the next-best opportunity available to them at the same level of risk. For instance, if you had $100,000 of your money tied up in the shares of XYZ, Incorporated, a corporation whose share price fluctuates greatly, your opportunity cost for that capital might be 14 percent—the return you'd be able to obtain for an investment of equivalent risk. Thus, for a big, stable corporation, the shareholders' opportunity cost might be 10 percent; for a risky, high-tech company, the owners might expect an 18 percent return.

The methodology for calculating the cost of capital for an individual business or for business units is beyond the scope of this book. Put simply, however, the cost of capital is the weighted average cost of the organization's different sources of capital.

From a practical standpoint, you might equate your company's cost of capital with the hurdle rate mentioned in our discussion of NPV. The CFO can provide this number, but will likely adjust the hurdle rate upward for projects of increasing risk.

What's a reasonable hurdle rate for a business? It varies from company to company. Typically, the hurdle rate is set well above what could be obtained from a risk-free investment, such as a U.S. Treasury bond. You can, in fact, think of the hurdle rate as this:

Hurdle Rate = Risk-Free Rate + Premium That Reflects the Enterprise's Risk

Like any investor, a business entity expects to be rewarded for the uncertainty to which it is subjected. And new product lines and other such activities are, by nature, filled with uncertainty. For this reason, they demand that prospective projects show particularly good promise.

Some companies use different hurdle rates for different types of investments, with low-risk investments having to clear a lower hurdle than that imposed on the higher-risk type. For example, a company might require that replacement of an existing assembly line or a specialized piece of equipment use a hurdle rate of 8 percent, whereas the expansion of an existing product line would have a 12 percent hurdle rate. The development of a new product line, which is riskier still, might require a 15 percent hurdle rate.

Sensitivity Analysis

Every business forecast includes one or more assumptions. In proposing the company's new coat-rack line, Amalgamated managers no doubt assumed that its dealers would pay X dollars per unit, that materials costs would be Y dollars per unit, and that the investment needed to get the operation off the ground would be Z dollars. These are just a few of many assumptions.

What would happen if one or more of these assumptions failed to hold? Sensitivity analysis helps you to ask just that question and to see the ramifications of incremental changes in the assumptions that underlie a particular projection.

Amalgamated expects its new line of coat racks to generate $70,000 in annual cash flow beginning a year from initiation of the project. But what if some variable in the scenario changed—how would it affect the overall evaluation of the investment opportunity?

Charles Peabody, the vice president of Amalgamated's Moose Head division, is projecting $70,000 in annual cash flow for five years—as in our initial present-value example. Natasha Rubskaya, the company's CFO, is less optimistic. She believes that Peabody has drastically underestimated the marketing costs necessary to support the new line. She predicts an annual cash stream of $45,000. Then there's Theodore Small, Amalgamated's senior vice president for new business development. Ever the optimist, he is convinced that the coat racks will practically sell themselves, producing an annual profit stream of $85,000 a year.

Amalgamated conducts a sensitivity analysis using the three profit scenarios. The NPV for Peabody's is $15,355. Rubskaya's is in negative territory at –$79,415. Small's scenario results in an NPV of $72,217.

If Rubskaya is right, the coat racks won't be worth the investment. If either of the other two is right, however, the investment will be worthwhile—and greatly worthwhile if Small's projections are on target. This is where judgment comes into play. If Natasha Rubskaya is the best estimator of the three, then Amalgamated's board of directors might prefer to take her estimate of the line's profit potential. Better still, the company should analyze its marketing costs in greater detail. Whichever route they take, sensitivity analysis will give the board of directors a more nuanced view of the investment and how it would be affected by various changes in assumptions. Other contingencies, or changes in other variables, could be mapped out just as easily.

The starting point for sensitivity analysis is in the underlying assumptions. If you are looking at breakeven analysis, take another look at your assumptions about each of the key critical components:

- **Fixed costs and variable costs.** Are you certain that your estimates for these costs are on target? Get the views of others on this, and try to establish a range of likely cost scenarios. Point estimates are almost always wrong.

- **Contribution.** The unit contribution is based on the selling price less the unit variable cost. Thus, if you're looking at a new product or service, chances are that the selling price is still to be tested. Question the validity of that assumption. If your product or service will be very similar to others already on the market, then the price that people are already paying may be a reliable guide. But if your product or service is "new to the world," then there may have been some guesswork involved in the determination of the selling price—even if your company conducted customer research. So again, it's a good idea to establish a range of likely selling prices for the new product or service.

You can perform the same type of sensitivity analysis on NPV calculations. In the Amalgamated case, for instance, you'd want to look more closely at the positive cash flows forecasted in years one through five. Most people cannot accurately forecast next year's cash flows, let alone those that occur many years in the future. So Charles Peabody's point forecast of $70,000 per year may not be reliable. Careful study may reveal a range of possible cash flows, with that range widening with each passing year, as shown here.

Year	0	1	2	3
Cash flow	−$250	+$68 to +$72	+$65 to +$75	+$62 to +$78

Year	4	5
Cash flow	$60 to +$80	+$58 to +$82

Again, you are much more likely to get it right if you forecast future cash flows as *ranges* of possible outcomes. Once you've determined them for your situation, calculate NPV for the best case, the worst case, and the most likely case. This will help your senior executives make a better decision. It will also help everyone understand which assumptions make or break the investment itself. These might be the selling price, the timing of the new product launch, or the cost of raw materials. Management can then focus its time and energy in making more accurate forecasts on those items, and once the project is in play, management will know that it must give those important points the greatest attention.

Economic Value Added

Our last tool is one that many corporations have adopted since the early 1990s. This tool gives shareholders and managers a better sense of business or business unit performance. Many use it as a metric for determining management bonuses. In many ways it is related to the

NPV and IRR concepts we've just covered. It's called *economic value added*, or EVA.

For many years, CEOs and unit managers would pat themselves on the back for producing income statement profits. "My company (unit) has produced yet another year of profitable operations," they would crow. They were big heroes. Financial consultants Joel Stern and Bennett Stewart blew the whistle on many of these executives in the late 1980s. Sure, these executives had produced accounting profits, but these were not *real* economic profits. And the reason for the discrepancy was a failure to recognize an important cost—the cost of the capital used in their operations.

Simply stated, EVA is net operating income after tax *less* the cost of the capital used to obtain it, or

EVA = Net Operating Profits after Taxes − (Capital Used × Cost of Capital)

By failing to account for the cost of capital, many businesses appear profitable even as they deplete shareholder wealth. But unless a business returns a profit greater than its cost of capital, it operates at a loss. It may pay taxes and report a profit on its income statement, but it destroys shareholder value if its gains are less than its cost of capital. And lots of seemingly profitable enterprises are doing just that. By taking all capital costs into account, including the cost of owners' equity, EVA calculates the monetary value that a business— or one of its operating units—creates or destroys in any given accounting period.

EVA is both a tool for evaluating new projects and a metric for gauging and rewarding managerial performance. In using it as an evaluation tool, we ask, "Will this project increase economic value?" By forecasting the impact of a new project or investment on net operating income after taxes (per our formula), and subtracting the cost of capital, we can determine its economic value added—or value lost. NPV does the same thing and, thanks to the discount rate, also recognizes the cost of capital. EVA is more effective, however, as a metric for measuring and rewarding management. It encourages managers to look at how capital is employed in their units and to ask, "Is this or that particular application of capital really returning at least its full costs?" They begin to take a hard look at assets that everyone customarily thought of as free goods: freight trains, machinery, buildings, assembly lines, and so forth. And they often discover that the company would be better off liquidating those assets and redeploying the proceeds into activities with higher returns.

Summing Up

This chapter has presented what many consider to be the most valuable financial tools available to business managers and analysts: net present value, internal rate of return, economic value added, and their various related concepts. These tools are far superior to payback and return on investment, which fail to recognize either the timing of cash flows or the firm's cost of capital (or hurdle rate). In brief, their characteristics are as follows:

- Net present value (NPV) is the monetary value today of a future stream of positive and negative future cash flows discounted at some annual compound interest rate. You can use NPV analysis for any number of decision-making purposes.

- Internal rate of return (IRR) is another tool that you can use to decide whether to commit to a particular investment opportunity, or to rank the desirability of various opportunities. IRR is the discount rate at which the NPV of an investment equals zero.

- Economic value added (EVA) is net operating income after tax less the cost of the capital used to obtain it. Many companies use EVA as a discipline to evaluate operations, investments, and business performance. Like NPV, it forces managers to take account of the cost of capital used in their decisions.

Whether you're considering the development of a new product, the purchase of a new asset, or any other type of investment, time-value tools can greatly enhance your decision-making ability. They can even help you determine the value of assets, a subject to which we turn next.

We've just skimmed the surface of this important subject in this chapter. If you wish to learn more about these topics, our advice is threefold: (1) read more about time-value concepts in any of the many corporate finance textbooks currently available; (2) learn how to use a financial calculator or financial spreadsheet programs; and (3) practice the application of these tools to business problems as you encounter them.

10

Valuation Concepts

Evaluating Opportunity

Key Topics Covered in This Chapter

- *Asset-based valuation methods*

- *Earnings-based valuation methods*

- *Discounted cash flow approach to valuation*

WHETHER YOU ARE buying or selling a global corporation, an operating division, a local restaurant, or a share of stock, the question, "What is its value?" outweighs most others, and for good reason. The rate of return from a good company or a good stock is likely to be disappointing if purchased at too high of a price. Likewise, underestimating the value of an entity in a sales transaction can leave plenty of the owners' money on the table.

Valuing an ongoing business—large or small—is neither easy nor exact. The field of finance, however, has developed methods for getting close to the value. This chapter will introduce you to several methods.[1]

But before we get started, consider several cautions. The true value of a business is never knowable with certainty. We may seek it, but we can never be sure that we have found the true value of the business. This lack of certainty is the result of two problems. First, alternative valuation methods consistently fail to produce the same outcome, even when meticulously calculated. Second, the product of valuation methods is only as good as the data and the estimates we bring to them, and these are often incomplete or unreliable. For example, one method depends heavily on estimates of future cash flows. In the very best cases, those estimates will only be close. In the worst cases, they will be far from the mark.

Another consideration is that a company is worth different amounts to different parties. Different prospective buyers are likely to assign different values to the same set of assets. For example, if you were a book collector who already owned first editions of every

Case Study: The Value of Hanging One's Hat

The first e-mail of the day has just hit your screen, and it's marked "Urgent." It is from your boss, the division general manager, and the CFO: "We'll be meeting tomorrow afternoon at 2:00 in the board room to discuss a possible acquisition of Amalgamated Hat Rack, Inc., which we believe would have a good strategic fit with our current home/office furnishings line. Please come prepared to discuss the valuation issues."

You're familiar with Amalgamated and its founder and CEO, Angus McDuff, whose story was featured in a recent issue of *Furniture Times*. It's likely that this same story spurred your company's interest in its possible acquisition. Given McDuff's age and given that his company is closely held by the McDuff family, key employees, and retired managers, you speculate that Amalgamated is ripe for a sale. This might be a good opportunity, but you are unsure of how to approach the valuation issues at tomorrow's meeting.

Hemingway novel except *For Whom the Bell Tolls,* then that book would be much more valuable to you than it would be to another collector who owned just one or two first-edition Hemingways. The reason? For you, the acquisition would complete a *set,* the value of which is greater than the sum of the individual volumes considered separately. Businesses look on acquisitions with a similar perspective. The acquisition of a small, high-tech company, for example, might provide an acquirer with the technology it needs to leverage its other operations. This explains, in part, why so many firms are bought out for more than the market value of their existing shares.

It is also important to keep in mind that valuation is the province of specialists. Small and closely held businesses typically turn to professional appraisers when their value must be established for purpose of the entity's sale, to determine the value of its shares when an employee stock ownership trust is used, or for some other purpose. When large, public firms or their business units are the subject of a valuation, executives generally turn to a variety of full-service accounting, investment banking, or consulting firms. Many of these vendors have departments devoted entirely to mergers and acquisitions, in which valuation issues are a central focus. Nevertheless, a well-rounded manager should understand the nature of different valuation methods—and their strengths and weaknesses.

Valuation problems often arise in the context of closely held businesses—that is, businesses with only a few owners—or in the sale of an operating unit of a public company. In neither case are there publicly traded ownership shares. Public markets for owner-ship, such as NASDAQ or the New York Stock Exchange, make value more transparent. Everyday buying and selling in these markets establishes a company's per-share price. And that price, multiplied by the number of outstanding shares, often provides a basis for a fair approximation of company value at a point in time.

Asset–Based Valuations

One way to value an enterprise is to determine the value of its assets. Here are four approaches to asset-based valuations: equity book value, adjusted book value, liquidation value, and replacement value.

Equity Book Value

Equity book value is the simplest valuation approach and uses the balance sheet as its primary source of information. Here's the formula:

Equity Book Value = Total Assets − Total Liabilities

To test-drive this formula, consider the balance sheet of Amalga-mated Hat Rack introduced in chapter 1. Table 1-1 showed that the total assets equal $3,635,000, whereas the total liabilities are $1,750,000. The difference—the equity book value—is $1,885,000. Notice that this is the same as total owners' equity. In other words, reduce the balance sheet (or book) value of the business's assets by the amount of its debts and other financial obligations, and you have its equity value.

This equity-book-value approach is easy and quick. And it is not uncommon to hear executives in a particular industry roughly calculating their company's value in the context of equity book value. For example, one owner might contend that his or her company is worth at least book value in a sale because that was the amount that he or she had invested in the business. But equity book value is not a reliable guide for businesses in many industries. The reason is that assets are placed on the balance sheet at their historical costs, which may not be their value today. The value of balance-sheet assets may be unrealistic for other reasons as well. Consider Amalgamated's assets:

- Accounts receivable could be suspect if many accounts are uncollectible.

- Inventory reflects historic cost, but inventory may be worthless or less valuable than its stated balance-sheet value (or "book" value) because of spoilage or obsolescence. Some inventory may be *under*valued.

- Property, plant, and equipment net of depreciation should also be closely examined—particularly land. If Amalgamated's property was put on the books in 1975—and if it happens to be in the heart of Silicon Valley—then its real market value may be ten or twenty times the 1975 figure.

The preceding are just a few examples. For many reasons, however, book value is not always true *market* value.

Adjusted Book Value

The weaknesses of the quick-and-dirty equity-book-value approach have led some to adopt *adjusted book value,* which attempts to restate the value of balance-sheet assets to realistic market levels. Consider the influence of adjusted book value in a leveraged buyout of a major retail store chain in the 1990s. At the time of the analysis, the store chain had an equity book value of $1.3 billion. Once its inventory and property assets were adjusted to their appraised values, however, the enterprise's value leaped to $2.2 billion—an increase of 69 percent.

When adjusting asset values, it is particularly important to determine the real value of any listed intangibles, such as goodwill and patents. In most cases, goodwill is an accounting fiction created when one company buys another at a premium to book value—that is, at a price higher than book value. The premium must be put on the balance sheet as goodwill. But to a potential buyer, the intangible asset may have no value.

Liquidation Value

Liquidation value is similar to adjusted book value. It attempts to restate balance-sheet values in terms of the net cash that would be realized if assets were disposed of in a quick sale and all liabilities of the company were paid off or otherwise settled. This approach recognizes that many assets, especially inventory and fixed assets, usually do not fetch as much as they would if the sale were made more deliberately.

Replacement Value

Some people use *replacement value* to obtain a rough estimate of value. This method simply estimates the cost of reproducing the business's assets. Of course, a buyer may not want to replicate all the assets included in the sale price of a company. In this case, the replacement value represents more than the value that the buyer would place on the company.

The various asset-based valuation approaches described here generally share some strengths and weaknesses. On the up side, the approaches are easy and inexpensive to calculate. They are also easy to understand. On the down side, both equity book value and liquidation value fail to reflect the actual market value of assets. And all approaches fail to recognize the intangible value of an ongoing enterprise, which derives much of its wealth-generating power from human knowledge, skill, and reputation.

Earnings–Based Valuation

Another approach to valuing a company is to capitalize its earnings. This involves multiplying one or another income statement earnings figure by some multiple. Some earnings-based methods are more sophisticated than others. There is also the question of which earnings figure and which multiple to use.

Earnings Multiple

For a publicly traded company, the current share price multiplied by the number of outstanding shares indicates the market value of the company's equity. Add in the value of the company's debt, and you have the total value of the enterprise. Think of it this way: The total value of a company is the equity of the owners *plus* any outstanding debt. Why add in the debt? Consider your own home. When you go to sell your house, you don't set the price at the level of your equity in the property. Its value is the total of the outstanding debt and your equity interest. Likewise, the value of a company is shareholders' equity plus the liabilities. This is often referred to as the *enterprise value.*

For a public company whose shares are priced by the market every business day, pricing the equity is straightforward. But what about the closely held corporation, whose share price is generally unknown, since such a firm does not trade in a public market? We can reach a value estimate by using the known *price-earnings multiple* (often called the *P/E ratio*) of similar enterprises that are publicly traded. The *price-earnings* approach to share value begins with this formula:

Share Price = Current Earnings × *Multiple*

We calculate the *multiple* from comparable publicly traded companies as follows:

Multiple = Share Price / Current Earnings

Thus, if XYZ Corporation's shares are trading at $50 per share and its current earnings are $5 per share, then the *multiple* is 10. In stock market parlance, we'd say that XYZ is trading at ten times earnings.

We can use this *multiple* approach to pricing the equity of a non-public corporation if we can find one or more similar enterprises with known *price-earnings multiples*. This is a challenge, since no two enterprises are exactly alike. The uniqueness of every business is why valuation experts recognize their work as part science and part art. To examine this method further, let's return to our example firm.

Since Amalgamated Hat Rack is a closely held firm, we have no readily available benchmark for valuing its shares. But let's suppose that we were successful in identifying a publicly traded company (or, even better, several companies) similar to Amalgamated in most respects—both as to industry and as to size. We'll call one of these firms Acme Corporation. And let's suppose that Acme's *P/E ratio* is 8. Let's also suppose that our crack researchers have discovered that another company, this one private, was recently acquired by a major office-furniture maker at roughly the same *multiple*: 8. This gives us confidence that our *multiple* of 8 is in the ballpark. With this information, let's revisit Amalgamated's income statement presented in chapter 1 (table 1-2) to find its net income (earnings) of $347,000.

Plugging the relevant numbers into the following formula, we estimate Amalgamated's value:

Earnings × *Appropriate Multiple* = Equity Value

$347,500 × 8 = $2,780,000

Remember that this is the value of the company's equity. To find the total "enterprise" value of Amalgamated, we must add in the total of its interest-bearing liabilities. Table 1-1 shows that the company's interest-bearing liabilities (short-term and long-term debt) for 2002 are $1,185,000. Thus, the value of the entire enterprise is as follows:

Enterprise Value = Equity Value + Value of Interest-Bearing Debt

$3,965,000 = $2,780,000 + $1,185,000

The effectiveness of the *multiple* approach to valuation depends in part on the reliability of the earnings figure. The most recent earnings might, for example, be unnaturally depressed by a onetime write-off of obsolete inventory, or pumped up by the sale of a subsidiary company. For this reason, it is essential that you factor out random and nonrecurring items. Likewise, you should review expenses to determine that they are normal—neither extraordinarily high nor extraordinarily low. For example, inordinately low maintenance and repair charges over a period of time would pump up near-term earnings but result in extraordinary expenses in the future for deferred maintenance. Similarly, nonrecurring, "windfall" sales can also distort the earnings picture.

In small, closely held companies, you need to pay particular attention to the salaries of the owner-managers and the members of their families. If these salaries have been unreasonably high or low, an adjustment of earnings is required. You should also assess the depreciation rates to determine their validity and, if necessary, to make appropriate adjustments to reported earnings. And while you're at it, take a hard look at the taxes that have reduced bottom-line profits. The amount of federal and state income taxes paid in the past may influence future earnings, because of carryover and carryback provisions in the tax laws.

EBIT Multiple

The reliability of the *multiple* approach to valuation we have just described depends on the comparability of the firm or firms used as proxies for the company whose value we seek to estimate. In the preceding Amalgamated example, we relied heavily on the observed *earnings multiple* of Acme Corporation, a publicly traded company whose business is similar to Amalgamated's. Unfortunately, these two companies could produce equal operating results yet indicate much different bottom-line profits to their shareholders. How is this possible? The answer is twofold: the manner in which they are financed, and taxes. If a company is heavily financed with debt, its interest expenses will be large, and those expenses will reduce the total dollars available to the owners at the bottom line. Likewise, one company's tax bill might be much higher than the other's for some reason that has little to do with its future wealth-producing capabilities. And taxes reduce bottom-line earnings.

Consider the hypothetical scenario in table 10-1. Notice that the two companies produce the same earnings before interest and taxes (EBIT). But because Acme uses more debt and less equity in financing its assets, its interest expense is much higher ($350,000 versus $110,000). This dramatically reduces its earnings before income taxes relative to Amalgamated. Even after each pays out an equal percentage in income taxes, Acme ends up with substantially less bottom-line earnings.

This earnings variation between two otherwise comparable enterprises would produce different equity values for the two, and would have to be reconciled by adding in the liabilities for each company. The problem can be circumvented, however, by using EBIT instead of bottom-line earnings in our valuation process. Some practitioners go one step further and use the EBITDA multi-

TABLE 10-1

Hypothetical Income Statements of Amalgamated Hat Rack and Acme Corporation

	Amalgamated	Acme
Earnings before Interest and Taxes	$757,500	$757,500
Less: Interest Expense	$110,000	$350,000
Earnings before Income Tax	$647,500	$407,500
Less: Income Tax	$300,000	$187,000
Net Income	$347,500	$220,500

ple. EBITDA is EBIT *plus* depreciation and amortization. Depreciation and amortization are noncash charges against bottom-line earnings—accounting allocations that tend to create differences between otherwise similar firms. By using EBITDA in the valuation equation, this potential distortion is avoided.

Discounted Cash Flow Method

One big problem with the earnings-based methods just described is that they are based on historical performance—what happened last year. And as the oft-heard saying goes, past performance is no assurance of future results. If you were making an offer to buy a local small business, chances are that you'd base your offer on its ability to produce profits in the years *ahead*. Likewise, if your company were hatching plans to acquire Amalgamated Hat Rack, it would be less interested in what Amalgamated earned in the past than in what it is likely to earn in the future under new management and as an integrated unit of your enterprise.

We can direct our earnings-based valuation toward the future by using a more sophisticated valuation method: *discounted cash flow* (DCF). The DCF valuation method is based on the same time-value-of-money concepts we covered in chapter 9. DCF determines value by calculating the present value of a business's future cash flows, including its terminal value. Since those cash flows are available to both equity holders and debt holders, DCF can reflect the value of the enterprise as a whole or can be confined to the cash flows left available to shareholders.

For example, let's apply this method to your own company's valuation of Amalgamated Hat Rack, using the following steps:

1. The process should begin with Amalgamated's income statement, from which your company's financial experts would try to identify Amalgamated's current actual cash flow. They would use EBITDA and make some adjustment for taxes and for changes in working capital. Necessary capital expenditures,

which are not visible on the income statement, reduce cash and must also be subtracted.

2. Your analysts would then estimate future annual cash flows—a tricky business to be sure.

3. Next, you would estimate the terminal value. You can either continue your cash flow estimates for twenty to thirty years (a questionable endeavor), or you can arbitrarily pick a date at which you will sell the business, and then estimate what that sale would net ($4.3 million in year 4 of the analysis that follows). That net figure after taxes will fall into the final year's cash flow. Alternatively, you could use the following equation for determining the present value of a perpetual series of equal annual cash flows:

Present Value = Cash Flow / Discount Rate

Using the figures in the illustration, we could assume that the final year's cash flow of $600 (thousand) will go on indefinitely (referred to as a perpetuity). This amount, divided by the discount rate of 12 percent, would give you a present value of $5 million.

4. Compute the present value of each year's cash flow using the technique described in the chapter 9.

5. Total the present values to determine the value of the enterprise as a whole.

We've illustrated these steps in a hypothetical valuation of Amalgamated Hat Rack, using a discount rate of 12 percent (table 10-2). Our calculated value there is $4,380,100. (Note that we've estimated that we'd sell the business to a new owner at the end of the fourth year, netting $4.3 million.)

In this illustration, we've conveniently ignored the many details that go into estimating future cash flows, determining the

TABLE 10-2

Discounted Cash Flow Analysis of Amalgamated (12 Percent Discount Rate)

	Present Value (in $1,000, Rounded)	Cash Flows (in $1,000)
Year 1	446.5	500
Year 2	418.5	525
Year 3	398.7	560
Year 4	381.6 + 2,734.8	600 + 4,300
Total	4,380.1	

appropriate discount rate (in this case we've used the firm's cost of capital), and the terminal value of the business. All are beyond the scope of this book—and all would be beyond your responsibility as a non-financial manager. Such determinations are best left to the experts. What's important for you is a general understanding of the discount cash flow method and its strengths and weaknesses.

The strengths of the method are numerous:

- It recognizes the time value of future cash flows.

- It is future oriented, and estimates future cash flows in terms of what the new owner could achieve.

- It accounts for the buyer's cost of capital.

- It does not depend on comparisons with similar companies— which are bound to be different in various dimensions (e.g., earnings-based multiples).

- It is based on real cash flows instead of accounting values.

The weakness of the method is that it assumes that future cash flows, including the terminal value, can be estimated with reasonable accuracy.

Summing Up

This chapter has examined the important but difficult subject of business valuation. It described three approaches:

- **Asset based.** The first valuation approach is asset-based: equity book value, adjusted book value, liquidation value, and replacement value. In general, these methods are easy to calculate and understand, but have notable weaknesses. Except for replacement and adjusted book methods, they fail to reflect the actual market values of assets; they also fail to recognize the intangible value of an ongoing enterprise, which derives much of its wealth-generating power from human knowledge, skill, and reputation.

- **Earnings based.** The second valuation approach described in this chapter is earnings-based: the P/E method, the EBIT, and EBITDA methods. The earnings-based approach is generally superior to asset-based methods, but depends on the availability of comparable businesses whose P/E multiples are known.

- **Cash–flow based.** Finally, we presented the discounted cash flow method, which is based on the concepts of the time value of money. The DCF method has many advantages, the most important being its future-looking orientation. This method estimates future cash flows in terms of what a new owner could achieve. It also recognizes the buyer's cost of capital. The major weakness of the method is the difficulty inherent in producing reliable estimates of future cash flows.

In the end, these different approaches to valuation are bound to produce different outcomes. Even the same method applied by two experienced professionals can produce different results. For this reason, most appraisers use more than one method in approximating the true value of an asset or a business.

Activity-Based Budgeting

Activity-based budgeting (ABB) is a new way of approaching the budgeting process. To understand ABB, we must first understand activity-based costing (ABC), which we touched on briefly in chapter 3. You can't do ABB unless your company has an ABC system.[1]

ABC is a new way to allocate the cost of resources consumed to the cost of objects such as products, customers, and distribution channels. Under traditional cost allocation, overhead costs are allocated to products using cost drivers such as direct labor hours and machine hours. These are referred to as volume drivers because these drivers vary proportionately with the total volume of output. The problem with traditional cost-allocation mechanisms is that they do not reflect that some costs are independent of the number of units produced in a batch. ABC, on the other hand, takes into account that smaller batches of a product are usually more expensive to produce than larger batches because of setup costs, even though the per-unit labor hours or machine hours might be the same for both batches.

Under ABC, the costs of resources such as rent, utilities, depreciation, and wages are first allocated to activities and then allocated from activities to cost objects using unit-, batch-, product-, customer-, and facility-level cost drivers. ABC looks at all the activities associated with producing something. An activity can be any event, task, or unit of work with a specified purpose. For example, the Moose Head Division of Amalgamated Hat Rack has operating activities such as the following:

- Purchase materials

- Prepare materials

- Schedule production

- Inspect products

- Package products

These operating activities are supported by management activities such as these:

- Hire new employees

- Train employees

- Manage computer network

- Manage payroll

- Prepare tax information

- Communicate with shareholders

Hierarchy of Activities

Managers can now look at how the activities fit together in a hierarchy. At the base are the unit-level activities required to produce one hat rack or to make one repair service call. For example, activities could include polishing the antlers, drilling holes in the antlers, and attaching the metal parts to the antlers. The number of unit activities performed is based on the production and sales volumes. At this level, the traditional cost-allocation methods based on labor hours, machine hours, or units produced work fairly well.

The next step up the hierarchy is the batch-level activities. These activities are performed for each batch. For example, Moose Head produces different models of antler hat racks. When it changes production from the standard upright to the hall/wall model, the activities for this batch might include handling the production orders, setting up the machines, and so forth. The resources required for these batch activities are unrelated to the number of units produced in the run or batch.

The traditional budgeting methods of allocating overhead costs based on direct labor hours or units produced don't necessarily relate to the actual resources used to perform the batch activities. This is an example of where activity-based costing and activity-based budgeting make a difference in the determination of costs and budget figures.

Similarly, farther up the hierarchy of activities, product-sustaining activities such as testing for quality or developing new products, or customer-sustaining activities such as providing individual customers with service, can be related to the current products, but their resource expenses can't be measured in terms of units produced or direct labor hours. Here again, assessing the resource costs for each activity gives a clearer picture of the overall costs of production.

Developing Cost Drivers

The real power behind ABC lies in understanding the cost drivers for each activity. The activity cost driver is a quantitative measure of the output of that activity. For example, for the activity of "setting up the machines," the cost driver is the number of setup hours. For the "schedule production tasks" activity, the cost driver is the number of production runs.

There are three basic types of cost drivers. By identifying which type of cost driver is associated with a particular activity, planners can measure the real resource expenses required for that activity.

- **Transaction cost drivers.** These drivers measure how often an activity is performed; for example, the number of machine setups or production runs or materials receipts.

- **Duration cost drivers.** These measure the amount of time an activity takes. For example, labor hours or setup hours may be the most accurate measure for activities involved with producing a certain product.

- **Intensity cost drivers.** These drivers charge for the resources used for an activity. If, for example, a customer service call requires a specialized technician to be available, then the real cost lies with the technician as a resource rather than the time involved for the call.

Once you've determined the cost drivers for each activity, you know what the activity truly costs. You can then use this information both for efficient operations and allocation of resources and for planning ahead—in other words, for budgeting.

From Activity–Based Costing to Activity–Based Budgeting

Derived from ABC methods, *activity-based budgeting* concentrates on the cost of resources required for producing and selling products and services. ABC starts with the cost of resources, allocates these costs to activities, and then allocates the cost of activities to products. Moving in the opposite direction, ABB starts with the planned product, sales volume, and mix and comes up with the required activities to produce that mix and volume. From these activities, budget planners can estimate the resources required and the cost of those resources. Thus, to use an ABB process, an organization needs to have historical data derived from an activity-based costing system. The information is then used to project the required cost of resources based on the anticipated product, volume, and mix.

The primary advantage of activity-based budgeting is that costs can be more accurately associated with activities, making the planning process more precise and corrections more effective. The disadvantage is that ABB can be costly and complex to establish—it may not be worth the trouble for a small company with few products or services. It also has to be adopted by and embedded into the whole organization; one division alone can't decide to develop its own ABC or ABB system. But when the circumstances are right, activity-based approaches to understanding the economic dynamics of an organization provide long-term planning benefits.

Notes

Chapter 2: Finding Meaning in Financial Statements

1. Our discussion of financial ratios leans heavily on William J. Bruns Jr., "Introduction to Financial Ratios and Financial Statement Analysis," Class note 9-193-029 (Boston: Harvard Business School Publishing, revised August 21, 1996).

2. Preferred stock or other securities that are convertible into common shares are often treated as common stock equivalents in making this calculation. We'll discuss these different classes of ownership and securities in chapter 4.

3. Robert S. Kaplan and David P. Norton, "The Balanced Scorecard: Measures That Drive Performance," *Harvard Business Review,* January–February, 1992. For a fuller discussion of the balanced scorecard and its implementation, see Robert S. Kaplan and David P. Norton, *The Balanced Scorecard* (Boston: Harvard Business School Press, 1996).

Chapter 3: Important Accounting Concepts

1. Our discussion of accounting for inventory is partly based on William J. Bruns Jr., "Accounting for Property, Plant, Equipment and Other Assets," Class note 9-193-046 (Boston: Harvard Business School Publishing, revised August 13, 1996).

2. This section is adapted from ibid.

3. H. Thomas Johnson and Robert Kaplan, *Relevance Lost* (Boston: Harvard Business School Press, 1987).

Chapter 4: Taxes

1. This section relies heavily on Michael J. Roberts, "The Legal Forms of Business," Class note 9-898-245 (Boston: Harvard Business School Publishing, revised August 27, 2001).

Chapter 5: Financing Operations and Growth

1. For the complete story of eBay's evolution, see David Bunnell (with Richard Luecke), *The eBay Phenomenon* (New York: John Wiley & Sons, 2000), pp. 17–30. All financial information about the company described here is from eBay's 2001 10-K form.

Chapter 6: Money and Capital Markets

1. Marcia Stigum and Frank Fabozzi, *The Dow Jones-Irwin Guide to Bonds and Money Market Instruments* (Homewood, Ill.: Dow Jones-Irwin, 1987), p. 6.

Chapter 9: The Time Value of Money

1. An NPV calculation determines the net present value of a series of cash flows according to the following algebraic formula:

$$\text{Net Present Value} = CF_0 + CF_1/(1 + i)^1 + CF_2/(1 + i)_2 + CF_n/(1 + i)^n$$

where each *CF* is a future cash flow, *n* is the number of years over which the profit stream is expected to occur, and *i* is the desired rate of return, or the discount rate. When you supply the values for each future cash flow, the discount rate, and the number of years, your spreadsheet or calculator will do the rest.

2. You'll get a slightly different number if you make the calculation on a financial calculator or spreadsheet program. The reason is a rounding error. Our PVIF goes to three decimal places, whereas calculators and spreadsheets generally go to higher decimal places.

Chapter 10: Valuation Concepts

1. This chapter has material adapted from Michael J. Robert, "Valuation Techniques," Class note 9-384-185 (Boston: Harvard Business School Publishing, revised August 18, 1988).

Appendix: Activity–Based Budgeting

1. The material in this appendix is from the "Budgeting" module of Harvard ManageMentor, Harvard Business Online Enterprise Solutions, Harvard Business School Publishing, available at <http://elearning.hbsp.org>.

Glossary

ACCOUNTS PAYABLE A category of balance-sheet liabilities representing moneys owed by the company to suppliers and other short-term creditors.

ACCOUNTS RECEIVABLE A category of balance-sheet assets representing moneys owed to the company by customers and others.

ACCRUAL ACCOUNTING An accounting practice that records transactions as they occur, whether or not cash trades hands.

ACTIVITY-BASED COSTING (ABC) An approach to cost accounting that carefully quantifies the links between performing particular activities and the economic demands those activities make on the organization's resources.

ADJUSTED BOOK VALUE A refinement of the book value method of valuation that attempts to restate the value of certain assets on the balance sheet according to realistic market values.

ALLOCATIONS See *indirect costs.*

ASSETS The balance-sheet items in which a company invests so that it can conduct business. Examples include cash and financial instruments, inventories of raw materials and finished goods, land, buildings, and equipment. Assets also include moneys owed to the company by customers and others—an asset category referred to as *accounts receivable.*

AVERAGE COST The average cost of inventory items is determined by adding the value of the beginning inventory and the total purchases made during the accounting period and dividing by the number of items.

BALANCE SHEET A financial statement that describes the assets owned by the business and how those assets are financed—with the funds of creditors (liabilities), the equity of the owners, or both. Also known as the statement of financial position.

BOND   A debt security usually issued with a fixed interest rate and a stated maturity date. The bond issuer has a contractual obligation to make periodic interest payments and to redeem the bond at its face value on maturity.

BOOK VALUE OF SHAREHOLDER EQUITY   A balance-sheet valuation method that calculates value as total assets less total liabilities.

BREAKEVEN ANALYSIS   A form of analysis that helps determine how much (or how much more) a company needs to sell in order to pay for the fixed investment—in other words, at what point the company will break even on its cash flow.

BUDGET   A document that translates strategic plans into measurable quantities that express the expected resources required and anticipated returns over a certain period. It functions as an action plan and presents the estimated future financial statements of the organization.

BURDEN   See *indirect costs.*

CAPITAL MARKETS   The financial markets in which long-term debt instruments and equity securities—including private placements—are issued and traded.

CASH-BASIS ACCOUNTING   An accounting practice that records transactions only when cash changes hands.

CASH BUDGET   A budget that predicts and plans for the level and timing of cash inflow and outflow.

CASH FLOW STATEMENT   A financial statement that details the reasons for changes in cash (and cash equivalents) during the accounting period. More specifically, it reflects all changes in cash as affected by operating activities, investments, and financing activities.

COLLATERAL   An asset pledged to the lender until such time as the loan is satisfied.

COMMERCIAL PAPER   A short-term financing instrument used primarily by large, creditworthy corporations as an alternative to short-term bank borrowing. Most paper is sold at a discount to its face value and is redeemable at face value on maturity.

COMMON STOCK   A security that represents a fractional ownership interest in the corporation that issued it.

CONTRIBUTION MARGIN   In cost accounting, the contribution by each unit of production to overhead and profits, or net revenue less direct cost per unit.

COST/BENEFIT ANALYSIS   A form of analysis that evaluates whether, over a given time frame, the benefits of the new investment, or the new business opportunity, will outweigh the associated costs.

COST OF CAPITAL   The opportunity cost that shareholders and lenders could earn on their capital if they invested in the next-best opportunity available to them at the same level of risk, calculated as the weighted average cost of the organization's different sources of capital.

COST OF GOODS SOLD   On the income statement, what it costs a company to produce its goods and services. This figure includes raw materials, production, and direct labor costs.

CURRENT ASSETS   Assets that are most easily converted to cash: cash equivalents such as certificates of deposit and U.S. Treasury bills, receivables, and inventory. Under generally accepted accounting principles, current assets are those that can be converted into cash within one year.

CURRENT LIABILITIES   Liabilities that must be paid in a year or less; these typically include short-term loans, salaries, income taxes, and accounts payable.

CURRENT RATIO   Current assets divided by current liabilities. This ratio is often used as a measure of a company's ability to meet currently maturing obligations.

DAYS RECEIVABLES OUTSTANDING   The average time it takes to collect on sales.

DEBT RATIO   The ratio of debt to either assets or equity in a company's financial structure.

DEPRECIATION   A noncash expense that effectively reduces the balance-sheet value of an asset over its presumed useful life.

DIRECT COSTS   Cost incurred as a direct consequence of producing a good or service—as opposed to overhead, or indirect costs.

DISCOUNTED CASH FLOW (DCF)   A method based on time-value-of-money concepts that calculates value by finding the present value of a business's future cash flows.

DISCOUNT RATE   The annual rate, expressed as a percentage, at which a future payment or series of payments is reduced to its present value.

DIVIDEND A distribution of after-tax corporate earnings to shareholders.

EARNINGS BEFORE INTEREST AND TAXES (EBIT) See *operating earnings.*

EARNINGS PER SHARE (EPS) A company's net earnings expressed on a per-share basis.

ECONOMIC VALUE ADDED (EVA) A measure of real economic profit calculated as net operating income after tax less the cost of the capital employed to obtain it.

ENTERPRISE VALUE The value of a company's equity plus its debt.

EQUITY BOOK VALUE The value of total assets less total liabilities.

FINANCIAL LEASE A lease that typically covers the entire useful life of the asset. The lease cannot be canceled unless the lessee makes all the scheduled payments. The lessee typically is required to pay for insurance, taxes, and the maintenance of the asset.

FINANCIAL LEVERAGE The degree to which borrowed money is used in acquiring assets. A corporation is said to be highly leveraged when its balance-sheet debt is much greater than its owners' equity.

FIRST-IN, FIRST-OUT (FIFO) A method of accounting for inventory that attributes the cost of goods sold to the cost of the oldest units of inventory.

FIXED ASSETS Assets that are difficult to convert to cash—for example, buildings and equipment. Sometimes called plant assets.

FIXED BUDGET A budget that covers a specific time frame—usually one fiscal year. At the end of the year, a new budget is prepared for the following year. A fixed budget may be reviewed at regular intervals—perhaps quarterly—so that adjustments and corrections can be made if needed, but the basic budget remains the same throughout the period.

FLEXIBLE BUDGET A budget whose revenues and costs can be adjusted, or flexed, according to the variances calculated between the budgeted amounts and actual product output and revenues.

FUTURE VALUE (FV) The amount to which a present value, or series of payments, will increase over a specific period at a specific compounding rate.

GENERALLY ACCEPTED ACCOUNTING PRINCIPLES (GAAP) In the United States, a body of conventions, rules, and procedures sanctioned by the Financial Accounting Standards Board, an independent, self-regulating body. All entities must follow GAAP in accounting for transactions and representing their results in financial statements.

GOODWILL An intangible balance-sheet asset. If a company has purchased another company for a price in excess of the fair market value of its assets, that "goodwill" is recorded as an asset. Goodwill may also represent intangible things such as the acquired company's excellent reputation, its brand names, or its patents, all of which may have real value.

GROSS MARGIN Sales revenues less the cost of goods sold. The roughest measure of profitability.

HURDLE RATE The minimal rate of return that all investments for a particular enterprise must achieve.

INCOME STATEMENT A financial statement that indicates the cumulative results of operations over a specified period. Also referred to as the profit-and-loss statement, or P&L.

INCREMENTAL BUDGETING A budgeting practice that extrapolates from historical figures. Managers look at the previous period's budget and actual results as well as expectations for the future in determining the budget for the next period.

INDIRECT COSTS Costs incurred that cannot be attributed to the production of any particular unit of output. Often referred to as overhead, allocations, or burden.

INITIAL PUBLIC OFFERING (IPO) A corporation's first offering of its shares to the public.

INTERNAL RATE OF RETURN (IRR) The discount rate at which the net present value of an investment equals zero.

INVENTORY The supplies, raw materials, components, and so forth, that a company uses in it operations. It also includes work in process—goods in various stages of production—as well as finished goods waiting to be sold and/or shipped.

INVENTORY TURNOVER The cost of goods sold divided by the average inventory.

IPO See *initial public offering.*

KAIZEN BUDGETING A budgeting method that incorporates continuous improvement into the budgeting process. Cost reduction is built into the budget on an incremental basis so that continual efforts are made to reduce costs over time. If the budgeted cost reductions are not achieved, then extra attention is given to that operating area.

LAST-IN, FIRST-OUT (LIFO) A method of inventory accounting that attributes the cost of goods sold to the most recently acquired units of inventory.

LIABILITY A claim against a company's assets.

LIQUIDITY The extent to which a company's assets can readily be turned into cash for meeting incoming obligations.

MARGINAL TAX RATE The percentage rate of tax paid on the next or last dollar of income.

MASTER BUDGET A budget that brings all operating budgets and the financial budget of an organization into one comprehensive picture. It summarizes all the individual financial projections of an organization for a given period.

MONEY MARKET The network of issuers and dealers through which large borrowers raise short-term money by selling their debt instruments. This network represents both new issues and secondary market trading.

NET EARNINGS See *net income.*

NET INCOME The "bottom line" of the income statement. Net income is revenues less expenses less taxes. Also referred to as net earnings or net profits.

NET PRESENT VALUE (NPV) The present value of one or more future cash flows less any initial investment costs.

NET PROFITS See *net income.*

NET WORKING CAPITAL. Current assets less current liabilities; the amount of money a company has tied up in short-term operating activities.

OPERATING BUDGET A projected target for performance in revenues, expenses, and operating income.

OPERATING EARNINGS On the income statement, gross margin less operating expenses and depreciation. Often called earnings before interest and taxes, or EBIT.

OPERATING EXPENSE On the balance sheet, a category that includes administrative expenses, employee salaries, rents, sales and marketing costs, as well as other costs of business not directly attributed to the cost of manufacturing a product.

OPERATING LEASE A lease whose term covers a portion of the asset's anticipated useful life. The lessor (the asset's owner) must typically renew the lease one or more times to recoup the cost of the asset and make a profit.

OPERATING EARNINGS Gross margin less operating expenses and depreciation. Also called earnings before interest and taxes, or EBIT.

OPERATING LEVERAGE The extent to which a company's operating costs are fixed versus variable. For example, a company that relies heavily on machinery and very few workers to produce its goods has a high operating leverage.

OPERATING MARGIN A financial ratio used by many analysts to gauge the profitability of a company's operating activities. It is calculated as earnings before interest and taxes (EBIT) divided by net sales.

OVERHEAD See *indirect costs.*

OWNERS' EQUITY What, if anything, is left over after total liabilities are deducted from total assets. Owners' equity is the sum of capital contributed by owners plus their retained earnings. Also known as shareholders' equity.

PARTNERSHIP A business entity with two or more owners and particular legal and tax characteristics.

PAYBACK PERIOD The length of time it will take a particular investment to pay for itself.

PLANT ASSETS See *fixed assets.*

PREFERRED STOCK An equity-like security that pays a specified dividend and has a superior position to common stock in case of distributions or liquidation.

PRESENT VALUE (PV) The monetary value today of a future payment discounted at some annual compound interest rate.

PROFIT-AND-LOSS STATEMENT (P&L) See *income statement.*

PROFIT MARGIN The percentage of every dollar of sales that makes it to the bottom line. Profit margin is net income after tax divided by net sales. Sometimes called the return on sales, or ROS.

REPLACEMENT VALUE A valuation approach that estimates the cost of reproducing an asset, rather than the more common reliance on an asset's book value.

RETAINED EARNINGS Annual net profits left after payment of dividends that accumulate on a company's balance sheet.

RETURN ON ASSETS (ROA) Relates net income to the company's total asset base and is calculated as net income divided by total assets.

RETURN ON EQUITY (ROE) Relates net income to the amount invested by shareholders (both initially and through retained earnings). It is a measure of the productivity of the shareholders' stake in the business and is calculated as net income divided by shareholders' equity.

RETURN ON SALES (ROS) See *profit margin*.

REVENUE The amount of money that results from selling products or services to customers.

ROLLING BUDGET A plan that is continually updated so that the time frame remains stable while the actual period covered by the budget changes. For example, as each month passes, a one-year rolling budget is extended by one month, so that there is always a one-year forward-looking budget in place.

SALE AND LEASEBACK A leasing arrangement in which an entity sells an asset to another (usually a financing company) to raise capital and then leases back that same asset.

SHAREHOLDERS' EQUITY See *owners' equity*.

SOLE PROPRIETORSHIP A business owned by a single individual.

SOLVENCY The ability to pay bills as they come due.

STATEMENT OF FINANCIAL POSITION See *balance sheet*.

TAX CREDIT A dollar-for-dollar reduction of tax liability.

TIMES INTEREST EARNED RATIO Earnings before interest and taxes divided by interest expense. Creditors use this ratio to gauge a company's ability to make future interest payment in the face of fluctuating operating results.

VARIANCE The difference between actual results and the results expected in the budget. A variance can be favorable, when the actual results are better than expected—or unfavorable, when the actual results are worse than expected.

VENTURE CAPITALIST (VC) A high-risk investor who seeks an equity position in a start-up or an early-growth company with high potential. In return for capital, the VC typically takes a significant percentage ownership of the business and a position on its board.

WORKING CAPITAL   See *net working capital*.

ZERO-BASED BUDGETING   A budgeting practice that begins each new budgeting cycle from a zero base, or from the ground up, as though the budget was being prepared for the first time. Each budget cycle starts with a critical review of every assumption and proposed expenditure. The advantage of zero-based budgeting is that it requires managers to perform a much more in-depth analysis on an annual basis of each line item—considering objectives, exploring alternatives, and justifying their requests.

For Further Reading

Accounting Concepts

For a discussion of accounting for inventory and the various approaches to depreciation, see William J. Bruns Jr., "Accounting for Property, Plant, Equipment and Other Assets," Case 9-193-046 (Boston: Harvard Business School Publishing, revised August 13, 1996).

For any question on cost accounting for managers, see Charles T. Horngren, George Foster, and Srikant M. Datar, "Cost Accounting: A Managerial Emphasis" (Upper Saddle River, NJ: Prentice Hall, 1997).

On the subject of activity-based cost accounting, see Robert S. Kaplan, "Introduction to Activity-Based Costing," Case 9-197-076 (Boston: Harvard Business School Publishing, revised July 5, 2001). This class discussion note will tell you what most managers need to know about ABC. Another useful and highly readable article on this subject is Robin Cooper and Robert S. Kaplan, "Profit Priorities from Activity-Based Costing," *Harvard Business Review,* May–June 1991.

Budgeting

Robert S. Kaplan and David P. Norton, "Linking Strategy to Planning and Budgeting," *Harvard Business Review,* May–June 2000, show how traditional budgeting practices can be made more responsive to a company's rapidly changing needs. The authors urge managers not just to focus on the operational budget, but to pay attention to the strategy budget as well, because the strategy budget is what finances the initiatives that facilitate company growth. Managers also need to avoid falling into the trap of thinking that initiatives are ends in themselves. Rather, initiatives are the means by which a company accomplishes its strategic objectives.

Charles T. Horngren, George Foster, and Srikant M. Datar, *Cost Accounting: A Managerial Emphasis* (Upper Saddle River, NJ: Prentice Hall, 1997), is a classic textbook on cost accounting. The book describes budgeting as a concept, a strategic tool, and a planning process in detail with examples and exercises. Not only is the treatment of budgeting thorough, but the topic is fully integrated into other cost accounting and planning material.

Financial Statements

For a concise treatment of ratio analysis, see William J. Bruns Jr., "Introduction to Financial Ratios and Financial Statement Analysis," Class note 9-193-029 (Boston: Harvard Business School Publishing, revised August 21, 1996).

For the subject of the balanced scorecard, go right to the source: Robert S. Kaplan and David P. Norton, "The Balanced Scorecard: Measures That Drive Performance," *Harvard Business Review,* January–February 1992. For a fuller discussion of the balanced scorecard and its implementation, see Robert S. Kaplan and David P. Norton, *The Balanced Scorecard* (Boston: Harvard Business School Press, 1996).

Money and Capital Markets

Marcia Stigum and Frank Fabozzi, *The Dow Jones-Irwin Guide to Bonds and Money Market Instruments* (Homewood, IL: Dow Jones-Irwin, 1987), remains one of the most accessible introductory sources on fixed-income securities and money market instruments. Stigum has written the authoritative volume on money market calculations (yields and pricing), and Fabozzi has produced several landmark books on fixed-income securities, but these are highly technical and suited to the interests of investment professionals.

For a straightforward description of various debt and equity securities, and the investor's perspective on them, Herbert B. Mayo's, *Investments: An Introduction,* 6th ed. (Fort Worth, TX: Harcourt/Dryden Press, 1999), is hard to beat.

Samuel L. Hayes III and Philip M. Hubbard, *Investment Banking: A Tale of Three Cities* (Boston: Harvard Business School Press, 1990), provide a highly readable history of investment banking and the development of money and capital markets in the three epicenters of global finance: New York, London, and Tokyo. The authors describe the historic role that investment banks have played in financing governments and industry and how that role as changed over the years.

Taxes

Weighing in at less than eight hundred pages of text, the *U.S. Master Tax Guide* (Chicago: CCH, 2002) is a good source on individual and business taxes. Revised annually, it has the most up-to-date information on tax rules and rates.

The Time Value of Money

Time-value concepts are among the most important you can master in becoming a better analyst and decision maker. We've presented the very basics in this book, but there's much more to learn. Any modern textbook on the principles of finance will include a chapter on this subject with many examples and exercises. Pick up one of these books, study the time-value chapter, and gain practice through the examples and exercises.

Valuation

The current bible on valuation is Tom Copland, Tim Koller, and Jack Murrin, *Valuation: Measuring and Managing the Value of Companies,* 2nd ed. (New York: John Wiley & Sons, 1995). This volume describes the valuation process and explains the differences between valuation and accounting practice. It illustrates how to maximize shareholder value, demonstrates how value-based management contributes to improved strategic thinking, and indicates how managers and different levels can add value.

For a short but less complete take on the subject, see Timothy Luehrman, "What's It Worth? A General Manager's Guide to Valuation," *Harvard Business Review,* May–June 1997. As Luehrman indicates, managers need to be able to value operations, opportunities (real options), and ownership claims. His article addresses all three. A reprint can be ordered directly from Harvard Business School Publishing's Web site: <http://www.hbsp.harvard.edu/home.html>.

Index

About the Subject Adviser

Samuel L. Hayes holds the Jacob H. Schiff Chair in Investment Banking, Emeritus, at the Harvard Business School. He has been involved in numerous aspects of the school's program, including teaching courses on Investment Banking, Management of Financial Services Organizations, and Corporate Financial Management. He has also chaired Harvard's International Senior Managers Program in Vevey, Switzerland, and taught in the summer Corporate Financial Management Program for senior finance executives and the Advanced Management Program and the Corporate Finance component in the School's Owner-President Management Program.

Professor Hayes' research has focused on capital markets and on the corporate interface with the securities markets. He has written numerous working papers and articles on related topics in such journals as the *Harvard Business Review*, the *Accounting Review*, the *Financial Analysis Journal,* the *Economic Review*, and *Financial Management*, and has contributed chapters to a number of books. Two articles that he coauthored on real estate finance won the Shattuck Award for the best article on real estate in 1967 and 1972. Professor Hayes is the coauthor or editor of seven books, including *Competition in the Investment Banking Industry* (Harvard University Press, 1983), *Investment Banking and Diligence* (Harvard Business School Press, 1986), *Wall Street and Regulation* (Harvard Business School Press, 1987), *Investment Banking: A Tale of Three Cities* (Harvard Business School Press, 1990), *Managing Financial Institutions* (The Dryden Press/HBJ, 1992), *Financial Services: Perspectives and*

Challenges (Harvard Business School Press, 1993), and *Islamic Law and Finance: Religion, Risk, and Return* (Kluwer Press, 1997).

Professor Hayes has consulted for a number of corporations, financial institutions, and government agencies, including the Justice Department, the Treasury Department, the Federal Trade Commission, and the Securities and Exchange Commission, where he served on the Tully Commission in 1994–1995 to examine compensation arrangements for stockbrokers. For twelve years, he was Chairman of the Finance Advisory Board of the Commonwealth of Massachusetts. He now serves on the Board of Managers of Swarthmore College and the Board of Trustees of the New England Conservatory of Music, and also serves on the Boards of the Eaton-Vance mutual funds, Tiffany & Company, Kobrick mutual funds, and Telect, Inc.

About the Writer

Richard Luecke is the writer of several books in the Harvard Business Essentials series. Based in Salem, Massachusetts, Mr. Luecke has authored or developed over thirty books and dozens of articles on a wide range of business subjects. He has an M.B.A. from the University of St. Thomas.